Encounters with Life

Too Many "Ah-Ha" Moments...and Still Counting

Vince Corozine

Vince Corozine Music - 2023

"With so little to make us smile or laugh, this book will lift your spirits and make your day" - Vince

Vince Corozine/Vince Corozine Music

Book Cover Design and Formatting: Mallory Rock, Rock Solid Book Design, www.RockSolidBookDesign.com

Concept for Book Cover Design, Illustrations Selection: Danae Crosley

Developmental Editor, Proofreading, Formatting: Joshua Rivedal

Book Layout: Joshua Rivedal

Encounters with Life: Too Many "Ah-Ha" Moments… and Still Counting/ Vince Corozine. -- 1st ed.
ISBN 978-1-7356171-2-1

Dedication

To my wife, Norma, who has been with me every step of this journey.
To everyone who added to my life experiences
and helped to enrich my life.
I would not have written this book without the urging of my children
Steve, Regina, and Matthew, who have always
made me laugh with joy!

Acknowledgements

Mom and Dad for their example of love, encouragement, and direction in my life.
My wife Norma for her inspiration and direction in everything I do.
My brothers Nick and Rich for their input and reassurance.
My children, Stephen, Regina, and Matthew
have been my "cheerleaders" during this process.
My granddaughter Danae Crosley for developing the concept for the cover design and for selecting the illustrations.
Reviewers:
Ray Blue saxophonist, composer, and educator in New York—performed with Kenny Baron, Houston Pearson, Bary Harris, Benny Powell, Eddie Henderson, The Sun Ra Arkestra; endorsed by Selmer and VanDorn Music.
Dr. William Brown, Professor and Research Fellow
at Regent University, Virginia Beach, Virginia.
Alan Goidel trombonist, teacher; performed with the Four Freshman, Tommy Dorsey, Glenn Miller, and Larry Elgart Bands.
Robbie Michaels, pianist, flutist, CEO of Pomposity International, California
Robert Hunt, pianist, flutist, CEO of Insurance Company

in San Francisco, CA.
Richard Lavsky, composer, conductor, and producer of music and sound design for television, radio, and theatrical motion pictures; composer of the movie, *Brighty of the Grand Canyon.*
Nick Savoca, director of Youth with a Mission, Florida.
Mary Mancini, international vocal artist and Mario Tacca, virtuoso accordionist New York.
Angelo Purcigliotti, saxophonist, Lions Club Carmel, Carmel, New York.
Tony Salvatori, arranger, educator, trombonist; performed with Buddy Rich and Herb Pomeroy Bands.
Dave Thomas, pianist, arranger, conductor.
Special thanks to Joshua Rivedal, for his editing, formatting, and adding a "touch of class" to my book.

Reviews

"This is the book to read for laughter, warmth, and a kind of musical education that does not require an instrument, practice, or learning your scales."

- *Robbie Michaels*

"Vince's wonderful, folksy, comedic writing style manages to combine George Carlin's understanding of life's elusive undercurrents with the somewhat absurd paraprosdokian (a phrase or observation with a totally surprising and unexpected ending) humor of Stephen Wright."

- *Richard Lavsky, composer, conductor, and producer of music and sound design for television, radio, and theatrical motion pictures.*

"Vince's recorded encounters with strangers and friends will not only make you laugh as you reflect on your own interactions with people, but his playful self-mocking will help you to learn how to laugh as you reflect on your own behavior."

- *Dr. William J. Brown, Professor and Research Fellow, School of Communication and the Arts, College of Arts and Sciences, Regent University, Virginia Beach, Virginia.*

"The "slice of life" format of Vince's book is perfect for busy readers. There are laughs on every page, so you can read as much or as little as you like in one sitting, and easily pick it up at any time without having to remember where you were in the story."

- *David Thomas, musician and retired music educator from New York State, currently residing in Arizona.*

It's obvious after reading his book, that throughout his life, Vince has always looked on the positive side of life and finds humor in every situation. He has definitely passed that on to the readers of his book!

- *Mary Mancini, international vocal artist; Mario Tacca, accordion virtuoso, organist, composer, arranger, and conductor*

"Vince has the uncanny ability to see humor and irony in life's daily occurrences! In doing so, he can see (and point out) the absurdities that lie within. That describes this book and its author perfectly."

- *Angelo Purcigliotti, lead tenor player with the Norm Hathaway Big Band since 1999.*

CONTENTS

Introduction

How many Americans sit in front of their TV screen watching *American Idol*, reality shows, *National Geographic* travel excursions, and the *Great Race,* longing for excitement and adventure to come our way? We sit with our bowls of popcorn, cheddar cheese balls, and potato chips on our laps as we yearn to meet fascinating people whose lives are exciting and without a doubt, are more fascinating than our own.

Encounters with Life is a narrative nonfiction book that presents a "tongue-in-cheek" look at contemporary culture. The book includes observations about the outlandish behavior of people whom I've met, whether it be at the mall during my daily walk, my travel experiences, time spent in the U.S. Army, or my days obtaining an education. The book has no plot, no rising action, no conflict, or even a climax. Ah, but it has characters.

Encounters with Life is a probing look at how times have changed, values have been compressed, and why people do such strange things...like wearing a ball cap backward on one's head.

After spending a good deal of time at the mall observing all types of people, I concluded that the "crazies" (those who react to life differently than I. The psychologically maladjusted with quirky idiosyncrasies) all walk in a clockwise direction, while I walk counterclockwise.

After all, racehorses rapidly speed away in a counterclockwise direction, as do NASCAR drivers and Olympic runners, as does the North Atlantic current. The planets in our solar system revolve around the sun in a counterclockwise motion, and the sun rotates using the same motion. Motors, car tires, hurricanes and tornados, and CDs rotate this way too. Most right-handed people (there are more righties than lefties) draw a circle using a counterclockwise motion. Why? The water in my bathtub revolves counterclockwise when draining. I want my life to be coordinated with the Earth and my bathtub. Don't you?

My goal was to make this, in part, a mini-inspirational book, motivating people who find themselves in an uncomfortable situation to persevere by using and creating opportunities for themselves.

Regardless of the roadblocks in my past, I was able to use my wit and ingenuity to follow my passion and become a working musician. When what seemed to be a bad experience appeared, I had the uncanny ability to turn an undesirable situation into a positive one. As doors closed for me, I went through another door or even a window. Making the best of a very mundane situation takes courage and ingenuity. I learned to "face the music" even when I didn't like the tune.

There's a saying, "It's hard to think of ways to drain the swamp when you're up to your neck in alligators." Refusing to be eaten and consumed by the situations at hand, I unwittingly assumed the M.O. of James Bond 007 and jumped on the backs of the alligators to survive the ordeal. By doing so, each experience led me to another, which eventually led me to where I am now.

I have neither credentials nor scientific certification upon which to rest my observations. This book is full of personal observations, nothing more. My curiosity has always been in the area of human behavior, and I am mystified and amazed at how or why people behave as they do.

Let the journey to meet all the interesting folk I've met on my *Encounters with Life* begin.

Part I

Mall Busters

My Mecca and Mental Health Resort

"At the height of laughter, the universe is flung into a kaleidoscope of new possibilities."

- Jean Houston

1

Let's Go Shopping

Human beings sometimes do foolish things… like writing letters to deceased or fictional characters. At Graceland in Memphis, Tennessee, as many as 100 Valentine cards addressed to Elvis Presley arrive each February. Sherlock Holmes receives more than 40 pieces of mail each week.

These aren't like the letters little children send to Santa Claus; they are from adults who use their valuable, fleeting time to send "dead letters" into oblivion.

Our view of life is often colored by our perspective, based on past experiences, and filtered through our prejudices.

One day, a man pulled into a service station to get gas. After the attendant washed his windshield, the man shouted, "It's still dirty; wash it again." So the attendant did. The man shouted again, "It's still dirty. Don't you know how to wash a windshield?" Just then, his wife reached over, removed his glasses, cleaned them, placed them back on his nose, and behold—the windshield was clean.

Speaking of interesting people, I've met more than a few of them at the mall. Why, as a man of a "certain age" have I been spending so much time at the mall? Exercise! Can this word truly be coming from someone like me? I love physical repose and inaction. I'm like millions of others who abhor exercise but need to do it to avoid getting a debilitating disease later in life.

Exercise comes in a variety of forms to suit different people: running, swimming, jogging, fencing, dancing, weightlifting, Pilates, playing sports, and walking. I'm exhausting myself just thinking of all the forms of exercise. I'll stick with walking, which is easy, convenient, and requires only two legs and a little bit of balance.

Thomas Jefferson said, "Walking is the best possible exercise." How could a man of his intellect and judgment be wrong? So walking it is.

Here's what motivated me to take such a drastic step in my life as walking.

One bright April morning, just as I was about to enter an Italian deli to purchase the daily newspaper, it suddenly appeared. A large apple turnover with a sugarcoated topping was sitting there in the deli window beckoning to me, "Eat me, take a bite." I did. I ate it all! Yikes, I was hooked!

While on vacation, a friend made a comment that sliced through me like a red-hot knife through butter. "If you can't see your belt, you're too fat!"

I quickly looked down for my belt, and I panicked—I couldn't see my feet, let alone my belt.

I never considered myself fat, chubby, or even portly in any way. However, as one gets older or more mature (I prefer that word), one's metabolism tends to slow, and a few extra pounds and inches show up where they don't belong or were never invited to appear in the first place. Unwelcome guests are always a bit of a problem. The Pennsylvania Dutch put it succinctly: "Fish and visitors both stink in three days." I was terrified that my inches would be like uninvited relatives who plan to spend forever in the guest bedroom.

That day, I weighed myself in at 217 pounds at six feet tall and felt okay with no noticeable loss of energy.

When I went for my yearly physical exam, my doctor told me that my cholesterol was a bit high and that I should lose about thirty pounds (maybe he couldn't see my belt either). He suggested that I take the prescribed medication for the cholesterol. In my mind, I immediately said, "no way."

So, I decided, right there and then, to begin a regime of walking and lose weight to lower my cholesterol numbers. I held a quick meeting with myself, and the verdict was unanimous; I would begin walking every morning, beginning tomorrow. I quickly eliminated sugary drinks and fruit juices too. Research shows that drinking one can of soda per day adds fifteen pounds to a person's frame in one year—no thanks!

I believe there's something about walking that keeps me young, too. If I go out for a good morning walk, forgetting my problems and worries, it will keep me alert and fresh and hopeful of fewer used notches on my belt.

Cicero stated, "It is exercise alone that supports the spirits and keeps the mind in vigor."

After all these years, can he still be right?

Determined, I always walk in the early morning because there is an accepted belief that the early morning is the best time for walking. Most folks are still sleeping or getting ready for work, while others are contemplating what they should do that day.

"An early morning walk is a blessing for the whole day." - Henry David Thoreau.

In a little over three months, I dropped seventeen pounds, lost two notches on my belt, and my cholesterol level plunged a whopping fifty points! And the best part of it all—no prescribed drugs were involved.

"Above all, do not lose your desire to walk. Every day I walk myself into a state of well-being and walk away from illness. I have walked myself into my best thoughts, and I know of no thought so burdensome that one cannot walk away from it." - Søren Kierkegaard.

My new diet now includes healthier foods that "pump up" my immune system, along with vitamins that sustain my vital organs, and best of all, I can now see my belt! Although I lost pounds, I quite unexpectedly gained a few new characters in my life at the mall (more on that a little later).

My interest peaked when I read an article estimating how a typical lifespan of seventy years is spent:

- Sleep: 23 years
- Work: 16 years
- Television: 8 years
- Travel: 6 years
- Leisure: 4.5 years
- Illness: 4 years
- Dressing and undressing: 2 years
- Religion: 0.5 years

I immediately noticed that exercise was absent from the listing. Why? I'm sure that this research was done long past the time Thomas Jefferson made his famous statement about walking. Which reminds me; it's time for a walk at… the mall!

2

Mall Culture

What strikes me most when I enter the mall is its cleanliness. Its shiny mirrors, clean sparking glass panels, amber-colored slate floor, and long inviting halls. The soft, fluffy armchairs, green potted plants, and thick rugs provide a quiet decorum. Nothing luxurious, though it is quite evident that funds were lavishly allotted to making the mall attractive. It's like a larger version of my living room.

I live about one and a half hours north of New York City in the rolling-hilled suburbs. There is a well-paved outdoor path near old railroad tracks in my town, used by many folks as a walking and bicycle path. Why don't I use this attractive and convenient outdoor path close to my home? Because a chorus of protestations always well up within me when thinking about it. *It is too cloudy to walk. It is too raw out. Looks like the weather calls for snow. Did I just hear rain outside?* Oh, and you have to dodge bicycles approaching from both directions, often without warning, that produce a gust of wind that almost knocks my hat from my head. And I'd have to avoid frisky, yappy dogs that think I'm their next meal (I read somewhere that 40 people are sent to the hospital for dog bites every minute). And don't get me started on the humidity.

The mall, in all its temperature-controlled glory, is a much better option for me, thank you very much. All the dogs are in cages in the pet store, and bikers are off-limits inside the mall.

"Hello, My Name Is Leonardo"

On a sunny Tuesday in May, I entered the mall through a series of double doors, and was greeted by a mysterious voice that said, "Hello, my name is Leonardo." I quickly glanced around and found that no one was there but me. "Hello, my name is Leonardo," the voice chirped again.

Upon closer investigation, I realized the voice was emanating from a photo machine. I was aghast! An inanimate object that talks—without a body, without a personality, and a soul. How depressing! The personalization of the moment was too much for me to handle. Antipathy arose within me almost to a hostile degree.

A voice without a face or a human body has always been a problem for me. I prefer to speak to a live person who can respond in kind as I query his or her mind. I certainly wasn't going to shout back to a machine!

My first thought was to escape quickly from the monster verbally assaulting me without my permission. I walked another lap around the mall, and again the inanimate object said, "Hello, my name is Leonardo," as if I didn't get it the first time.

I have never been one prone to violence or antagonistic fits of rage, but I came close on this Tuesday morning in May at about 7:45 a.m. Thoughts of rage and pulverization quickly came to mind, but I wisely decided not to bash the machine since Rocco, the macho security guard, would probably arrest me, and I would be required to pay a stiff fine for my uncontrollable outburst. Then another thought, even more horrifying than the first struck me. The machine would most likely be replaced with one that said, "Hello, my name is Francis."

Immigrants Are Great Listeners

Whirling brushes of soft feathers dusted everything within reach. Workers decked out in maroon mall shirts with dusters in hand populate the mall in the early morning hours. I see them working fervently sweeping floors, washing benches, cleaning windows and glass panels, and making the mall sparkle like a brand-new kitchen.

These workers are quiet, unassuming folks who seldom look me in the eye, but continue to work, even when I bring forth a cheery, "Good morning." Every day I see Pablo, an immigrant to the U.S., working and cleaning windows with satisfaction and well-deserved pride. He waves, smiles, and nods his head as I say, "Good morning."

If I say, "Nice day," he nods and smiles.

If I say, "It's cold, and it's raining," he nods and smiles. I guess he likes all kinds of weather. To test my theory, I should tell him a hurricane is on its way, the river is rising, and the wind velocity is increasing to over 200 miles per hour. Would he then nod and smile?

One morning I watched as Pablo was leaning forward on his broom; he stopped and stared at the mall manager, who unexpectedly emerged from a dark corner. How strange and a little creepy!

THE BOSS

The mall manager is a close-shaven man with a sandy complexion and a somewhat rosy-colored nose, and often wears a blue shirt and a gold tie. He is a heavy-set man (who looks like he never exercises) and seems to be carrying the weight of the world on his shoulders. He appears to be a stern man with an unhappy nature.

I couldn't help but stare as the scene with the mall manager and Pablo unfolded.

The manager suddenly screamed at Pablo, and his face turned grape purple. His ears stuck out as he hiked his shoulders up, making it look like he didn't have a neck. His snarled eyes flashed, and his tongue extended like a lizard's.

A bit taller than Pablo, the manager puffed out his chest, pulled his shoulders back, and began to bark orders at timid Pablo, who smiled and nodded as he listened to the verbal assault. Despite his small stature, Pablo demonstrated great dignity as he weathered his boss's tirade.

The manager is a bully of a man, no doubt driven to the point where the ends justify the means, screaming to get his point across rather than trying to have a conversation. To this man, the product or bottom line is all-important and takes precedence over human relationships. I prefer to approach life with a passion—where one enjoys everything on the way to achieving results.

Pablo, I would imagine, is the same way. But I suppose I should ask him sometime. Maybe he'd just smile and nod. That Pablo is an agreeable fellow.

3

Clockwise or Counterclockwise

The most startling thing I notice as I walk through the mall these days, are the people who appear to be "eccentric" and walk the mall in a clockwise direction, while I walk counterclockwise! There is true creative predictability surrounding each of the characters.

There are two kinds of folks: the normal ones and the "crazies." The "crazies" respond somewhat differently than I do in most situations. They also have a small quirk in their personalities that makes them stick out in a crowd if one is observant and perceptive enough to notice.

I worked out a theory of my own on the subject. Oh yes, "crazies" seem to have one thing in common; they walk the mall in a clockwise direction, while I, and the other so-called normal folk, walk in a counterclockwise direction.

I wonder if there is any connection between mental quirks and walking clockwise. My educational degrees are all in music, so I cannot positively say there is any connection between them. Everything I learned about people I gleaned from observation, reading, traveling, and asking questions. Should I attempt to walk clockwise to see if there is any difference?

As I write this, something inside me bravely cries, "No! I am not willing to take that chance!"

SUPERMAN

Rocco is one of the most focused and intense members of the mall family I now belong to. He is a macho security guard whose muscles protrude and expand well beyond his shirt. He stands about five feet eight inches tall with a stocky, muscular build. He wears an imposing hat that resembles those worn by New York State Troopers.

He is a friendly, amiable fellow who speaks to everybody and openly shows respect for those who are older than he.

Rocco enters and competes in bodybuilding contests and soon anticipates turning professional. He lifts weights and is a self-proclaimed expert regarding healthy foods, anatomy, exercise, and vitamin supplements.

"Did you know that the human heart creates enough pressure when it pumps out of the body to squirt blood 30 feet?" He once blurted out while we discussed some of his favorite topics.

"Wow, that's an eye-opener," I replied, unsure of how to respond to a factoid like that.

"Yeah, and banging your head against a wall uses 150 calories an hour."

"Great, but I don't think I'll try that one. I may have to buy lots of pain medicine."

He laughed heartily and replied, "How about this one…a flea can jump 350 times its body length. It's like a human jumping the length of a football field."

"That one I can use for sure," I said.

Rocco knows many facts about the workings of the human body. I'm not a smoker, and one day, I asked Rocco if he ever smoked.

"I did once in junior high school but quit soon after that when I got into lifting weights. I heard that a pack-a-day smoker will lose approximately two teeth every ten years," he remarked.

I was glad I don't smoke and still have all my teeth.

He occasionally wins bodybuilding contests in New York and Florida. He told me that he is on a very stringent diet, eating twelve small meals a day comprised of tilapia and hand-washed chicken. He asks the girls at the fast-food outlets to wash the chicken of all chemicals. He also works out under the tutelage of a world-class trainer. His aim and strategy are to accumulate enough money with his bodybuilding contest winnings so he can begin his own business.

Rocco has a keen eye for the ladies and likes to chat with them. I like the fact that he has an old-fashioned chivalrous respect for women. He speaks in a rumbling, resonant, bass voice with the scratchiness of sandpaper.

Rocco's presence is both reassuring and intimidating. I certainly admire his spirit, determination, and fortitude. And if the security guard thing or the bodybuilding thing doesn't work out, he may have a future as a professional Jeopardy contestant.

4

The "Normals"

Life Without a Cell Phone

I must be the only person on the planet who doesn't have a cell phone. It appears as though I am a reactionary who believes that talking on the phone is to convey or collect information, rather than to take up time with worthless, nonsensical, unessential chatter.

Nor do I feel a need to call home and inform my wife that I will be detained for another fifteen minutes. I think her world can continue nicely without that tidbit of information.

On a warm Thursday morning in June, while driving to the mall at 7:30 a.m., a woman driving an SUV was tailgating me while chatting on her cell phone. This is a typical scenario in New York, even with the statute outlawing cell phone usage in moving vehicles.

Some folks listen attentively and assiduously to their iPods as they walk the mall, almost impervious to the fact that others are around them. A screeching car or bus could race toward them, and they wouldn't know it until it is too late. I don't have the time to listen to a thousand songs on an iPhone, let alone download them. That would mean that for me to listen to all 1000 in one month, I would have to listen to thirty-three songs per day.

I am a selective consumer when it comes to listening to music. I carefully select what I wish to listen to and then choose to concentrate on it and nothing else. I abhor using music as a background for another activity. When this happens, it is too easy to tune the music out. I prefer to listen attentively to the musical sounds as they emanate from a live orchestra or my CD player. The choice of using music as a background for another activity or concentrating on it reminds me of the old song, "Something's Gotta Give." You can't concentrate on two matters at one time unless, of course, you have two heads.

STATISTICIAN

Al, a lean man in his early seventies, looks rather frail and doleful. Perhaps his life was a difficult one. He appears to sit alone day by day. One day he looked lonely and listless, with a nasty, irritating cough. I noticed he had several of his upper and lower teeth missing. I guess he had a difficult life and can't afford to fix his teeth. I assume he lives alone because his tan jacket is badly soiled. If Al had a wife, she would no doubt make sure his jacket was clean. He most likely lives in a small, dreary apartment with a television set and radio, and follows all the sporting events. No doubt, Al survives on a meager allowance from Social Security. These are all assumptions on my part.

Al waits for the deli to open at 9 a.m. and orders an English muffin with strawberry jam and coffee every day! I wonder if he enjoys sitting alone while eating. I had to find out.

"Good morning," I said, interrupting him before a big bite. "Nice breakfast you're having."

"Yeah, I eat this every morning; it's good for my liver," he replied.

"Do you have problems with your liver?"

"No, it works just fine."

He frowned at his English muffin and ate it slowly, as though he wished to convey the impression that the process hurt him more than it hurt the muffin.

I make it a practice of saying hello to Al every morning as he bites into his English muffin.

I soon discovered that Al is an avid sports fan who closely follows the Yankees and the Mets. Every day he doles out the latest scores, batting averages, plays of the day, and which players committed errors.

On a Tuesday morning, he asked, "Who hit a base hit for two different teams in the same doubleheader?"

"I don't know that one, Al," I said.

"Joel Youngblood got a hit for the Mets in the first game; then between games of the doubleheader, he was traded to the Giants whom the Mets were playing, and in the second game, he got a hit for the Giants."

"Amazing fact, Al," I said, not remembering who Joel Youngblood was. Before he could tell me, I quietly smiled, waved, and continued walking.

While reading my Sunday newspaper, I noticed a glossy photo of a NY Yankee player. My first thought was that Al would like to have it. The next day, I handed the photo to him enclosed in a clear manila envelope. He opened it carefully and smiled. "He's a good player."

"The picture is for you," I replied. His countenance brightened, and he beamed as though I had given him a hundred-dollar bill. I saw him the next morning carrying the envelope. A little caring matters.

I am indeed fortunate to have a friend like Al. Thanks to him, I no longer have to purchase a newspaper, watch a baseball game on television, or check the scores on the New York radio stations. Instead, I can read, write music, listen to CDs, practice my saxophone, and watch movies.

VETERAN

He is a short-legged, long-bodied, thin, but healthy-looking nonchalant, affable man in his sixties with a large sandy head of hair. He has a mischievous grin and a prominent Brooklyn accent. Charlie, another of my fragmented but lovable mall family, is a friendly guy with a placid nature, who often ambles around the mall, peering into the store windows.

On this day, for several minutes, he began walking in a large semicircle and then stopped at the deli to grab some breakfast. He sat by himself with a cup of coffee and a wooden stirrer, sipping, stirring, and reading the newspaper.

"Charlie, how much coffee do you drink every day?" I asked.

"Too much!" he answered, "About six cups."

"You like coffee, eh?"

"No, I don't like it at all," he replied with a smirk.

"Then, why do you drink it?"

"Oh, my favorite movie stars, Humphrey Bogart and Robert Mitchum drank it."

I nodded as though I understood his logic and responded, "Oh, I see."

He displays an acute vividness of a war-scarred veteran remembering the time he was in World War II. Charlie's sense of humor and good nature. I often make short, terse, and somewhat humorous remarks to him whenever we meet up.

"Did you hear that Christopher Columbus was wrong?" I asked.

"He was?" he exclaimed, surprised.

"He said that the world was round."

"It isn't?"

"The world isn't round; it's crooked!" I replied.

A flickering smile crossed his face. He laughed and snickered simultaneously.

Charlie leaned toward me and said, "Did you know that Maine is the only state whose name is just one syllable?"

I immediately began to review the names of all the states, and by golly, he was right.

Another day Charlie stopped me and told me what he just read in the newspaper. "Did you realize the average American over 50 will have spent five years waiting in lines and six months waiting at red lights?"

"I am astonished. Is there anything we can do about it?" I asked.

He shrugged his shoulders, smiled, and laughed softly as he carefully folded his newspaper and tucked it under his arm. He continued on with his hands in his pockets as he slowly shook his head. I continued my counterclockwise walk around the mall.

How I envy Charlie. He looks as though he could eat tons of food and never gain a pound. Thousands of veterans like Charlie walk malls, sip coffee, and go unnoticed and unappreciated.

5

Primal Hunger

There he was, sitting on a sofa beside a gigantic green potted plant; the man was almost as wide as the potted plant. He started to remove his jacket but changed his mind. His thick fingers smudged the brown paper bag. He dropped his can of soda on the floor, where it bounced twice before landing at his feet.

"May I help?" I asked.

After thirty seconds of silent pondering, he looked at me with a faint smile and nodded his head.

I leaned over to pick up the can of soda and handed it to him. He again nodded his head and smiled. He tried to rise from the couch, but with all his size, he was very weak. He looked like a lame hippo caught in a trap. I sat beside him and watched as he mellifluously consumed a large burger with everything on it, large fries, and a diet soda (I guess the diet soda was supposed to wash away calories).

He then snapped the lid, held the soda can up to his already open mouth, and chugged all of it without once coming up for air. It was an amazing thing to see! He gulped his soda as though it was the last one on earth.

I paid considerable attention to him and noticed how difficult it was for him to breathe as he gingerly rose from the sofa.

Then came the waiting. For one thing, he didn't know what to do with his hands—-he thrust one of them nervously over his knee. As he chewed his nails, he started shifting slowly from one foot to the other as he paced and balanced himself. He considered taking some gum from his shirt pocket, decided against it, and wobbled uncomfortably some more.

He sat down, leaned back with his hands across his chest, and belched, then loosed his belt and grunted as he began to pick his teeth with a gray, plastic toothpick.

By this time, my attention had been completely engrossed by the situation. I couldn't help thinking that he looked like an oversized container of Jell-O with a belt.

He casually reached up and rubbed his chin, from which drops of food leftover from his morning snack fell gently to the floor.

All at once, he began to walk, pacing slowly back and forth. He had to steady himself with one hand set firmly on the couch, and his breathing could be felt from across the hall. Exhausted by so stupendous an effort, he could do nothing else.

He rubbed his face in his hands, and worn out by his exertions, he gave a low cry of despair and staggered to a nearby water fountain, where he drank himself into a gross stupor.

THE THREE TENORS

One group of mall friends consists of retired men of Italian descent. I fondly call them the "The Three Tenors" and so aptly named them Pepperoni, Prosciutto, and Provolone. They are exceedingly good-humored and affable. They seem to enjoy each other's company during their daily tour of the mall. They are friendly, funny, and fascinating. They wave to me and enjoy the occasional witty one-liners I toss at them.

For instance: A guy went to see his dentist and asked, "Hey doc, I have a yellow tooth. What do I do?" The dentist answered, "Wear a brown tie!"

The response from the Italian trio is immediate laughter, and I get multiple responses in Italian. I once asked them why they walk in the morning and not in the afternoon. After all, they are retired and could sleep late.

The large one whom I refer to as "Provolone," muttered, "Your feet are bigger in the afternoon than at other times of the day, and it would be too much of an effort."

Another inconsequential fact penetrated my puny brain.

They must have gone on laughing for quite a time, as though they put one over on me. I don't know if what they told me was true or not, but I didn't want to expend the time to research it and find out either. If it were true, then questions about when to purchase a pair of shoes or sneakers would come into play. Maybe that's why some people's feet hurt. Before asking for further explanations, I hurriedly walk on in my quest to lose weight.

BUXOM BEAUTIES

Four generously proportioned women in their late fifties and early sixties walk the mall almost every day. All are in dire need of exercise with their large rear expanses and hunched, rounded shoulders. They look like they are built for comfort rather than speed. I believe people look much better if they do not stare at the ground when they walk. They should look up as though they are leading a marching band (notice how my musical background creeps in).

One lady jabbers on continuously on her cell phone as she walks, totally unconcerned about the other three friends nearby. She prattles on for about thirty minutes of my walk. The only time I can remember being on the phone for thirty minutes was when I had to wait twenty-eight minutes for the person on the other line to pick up the phone. How can someone babble on for thirty minutes straight? Another lady dons a baseball cap that matches every pair of slacks she wears. A real high-fashion mall buster.

Unlike the Three Tenors, they chatted constantly about their problems and gossiped about their "friends".

They are so absorbed in tepid conversations that they are unaware of others around them. If somebody fainted in their path, they would no doubt step over the body and continue walking and talking as before.

Whenever I utter a cheery, "Hello," I receive no response. No doubt they don't want to be interrupted, or maybe they hate men?

After walking for about thirty minutes, the Buxom Beauties amble toward a fast-food outlet and order a big breakfast. All that walking must have worked up an appetite.

One day, while I was sitting at a table eating an English muffin with currant jelly on it, I overheard the Buxom Beauties gossiping at a table near mine. Now, mind you, I do not eavesdrop on the conversations of others, but their voices projected, so I could not avoid hearing what they were saying. After a bit of polite small talk, the largest and loudest of the group announced, "My, isn't he cute," while gazing at Rocco, the weightlifter security guard who was talking to a pretty young girl in front of one of the food outlets.

"I wonder if he's married or has a girlfriend."

"Yes, he's a darling," another echoed.

"Indeed, he is," authenticated the third generously proportioned woman.

"He seems like such a nice man," whispered the second woman. "Such energy and masculinity. I wish my husband looked like him."

They all snickered like young schoolgirls out on the playground at lunchtime.

"I just want to reach out and pinch his iddy-biddy muscles!" emoted lady number three.

By now, I could no longer stand the punishment of frivolous small talk; I feared I would have to run into the bathroom and vomit. Therefore, I quickly rose from my less-than-comfortable chair to continue walking, as I shook my head in disbelief over what I just heard.

DASHING GENTLEMAN

He wears a neatly tailored brown suit with pinstripes, brown-laced shoes, white socks, and a yellow straw hat. He is quite a sight to see. He shuffles slowly and deliberately due to his frail condition. He walks as though he has a load in his pants like a baby in squishy diaper trots. Or maybe he has a bad case of hemorrhoids.

I am greeted by a friendly wave and a smile as I return my ebullient, "Hello."

He walks so slowly and deliberately that I often pass him three or four times during my twelve laps of the mall. (Remember, I am walking counterclockwise). He inches along with the dignity and charm of one who is ice-skating in slow motion or as a drum major leading a marching band in slow motion as it plays a stately but unhurried Sousa march.

Mr. Witherspoon grins a little in a sly way as he keeps his gaze straight ahead while he walks. He only moves the lower half of his body, somewhat like an Irish folk dancer, with the top part of his body staying somewhat rigid. He is a remarkable sight.

BABY BRIGADE

On any morning at the mall, numerous folks are walking, talking, or squawking about the weather.

One captivating event is the Baby Brigade.

Here is a collection of about ten or twelve young mothers in their twenties with babies sitting in a stroller, who are led by an enthusiastic, effervescent aerobics instructor.

Without a doubt, the mothers are here to benefit from exercising under the scrutiny of the lively and spirited aerobics instructor.

The baby carriages are lined in a row with the babies facing the aerobics instructor, who barks commands such as "Lift your leg!" "Bend your knees 1, 2, 3, 4," "Squat 20 times 1, 2, 3, 4," and other such grueling directions.

The aerobics instructor has the mothers jumping over and around bright red plastic objects and pulling on black stretch ropes that extend six feet. While the mothers are huffing and puffing, the babies are looking on in disbelief, usually screaming at the top of their lungs. They are no doubt providing competition with the energetic aerobics trainer along with ringing cell phones.

After about thirty minutes of stretching, straining, sweating, and swaying exercises, a Baby Train is formed. The mothers line up single-file behind each other with their baby carriages in front of them. The animated instructor bellows a command, and she hurriedly begins to run ahead of them. This Baby Train of running mothers with strollers encircles the mall for about fifteen minutes. I shudder to think of what might happen if any of them stopped short. There would be a baby collision of the worst kind!

As I carefully and quietly walk around this contingent of exercising addicts, the disciplined and gruff aerobics trainer smiles at me. I try not to smile back as she might think I may be interested in joining her group. Egads! The thought of that is nauseating! If I did manage to do some of the exercises, I would never be able to get up again!

I continue walking as the booming voice of the instructor echoes throughout the mall.

6

THE "CRAZIES"

Yes, they all walk clockwise around the mall, every one of them!

THE ROADRUNNER

I'm talking to the Italian trio when a small, brawny man, Leo, with cat-like ease of carriage, comes striding into the mall, rubbing his hands as he walks. Leo saunters to a corner of the mall, with a commanding gait, just outside of one of the large anchor department stores. He stands gazing at the open hallway, a bit like a prancing stallion at the starting gate.

Suddenly, with great panache, he charges forward and takes off like a super-charged NASCAR driver just beginning a race. Instantly, he displays the vigor of a well-tuned healthy young machine as he furiously pumps his arms and bobs his head in an up-and-down motion as he thrusts his body forward, vigorously blowing air through his puffy cheeks. In his hands, he has a brown, oval-shaped weight, which reminds me of a bulky dog bone. On his head, he has a pair of headphones. No doubt, he is listening to one of the thousand songs on his iPod.

No one dares to get in his way as he propels his arms back and forth with machine-like precision. He whizzes by. As he passes me for the third time, going clockwise, the breeze created by his passing is refreshing. Leo walks faster than anyone in the mall.

FRENZIED FREDA

Freda is a pallid frightened girl with a slight frame and a pasty complexion. A peculiar beeswax tint on her hair is noticeable, her head drooping as she walks. She drapes a red woolen shawl over her head and around her neck.

The figure and gait of the girl are young, but youth is absent from her face. In addition, looking at her frightened face one might suppose that the ceiling had fallen on her or she had just seen a ghost in the mall. When she walks, she toddles along, taking short, uncertain steps with an abrupt glide. It is most unusual. I pass her many times as I walk counterclockwise, and she, clockwise. I am apprehensive about looking her in the eyes or saying hello, fearing she might think I was trying to assault her.

BOUNCING BURT

Bouncing Burt bounces up and down when he walks. He has an affinity for making small talk. He is an amiable young man in his thirties, who speaks and waves to everybody—as he walks clockwise around the mall.

One day Bouncing Burt stopped to talk to me, "Hi Vince, did you know that I'm left-handed?" he inquired.

"No, I didn't know that. Is it important?" I replied.

"Yeah, only six percent of the population are lefties, and I'm one of them."

"Congratulations, Burt." I hastily shook his hand. "I didn't know that either."

"Did you know that all polar bears are left-handed like me?" he asked.

I thought about the fact that right-handed people live, on average, nine years longer than left-handed people. I wonder if an ambidextrous person gets to split the difference. I also wonder if polar bears switched hands would they live longer?

"Where did you find that out?" I remarked.

"From a TV program," he replied.

"I guess if you're left-handed, then you must be related to a polar bear."

Burt laughed heartily and shook his head, "No. But the polar bears are smart, just like me."

"So, I've heard. Good for you, Burt…but remember to stay off the ice."

He let out a good-natured chuckle and ambled down the long mall hall.

Another time Burt blurted out, "Vince, look at the new pair of sunglasses I just bought."

"Nice glasses, Burt," I replied.

"I bought them for ten dollars," he said.

"Say, you got a good deal."

"The man told me that these are real designer glasses, too. Look at the sticker in the right corner," he exclaimed.

Thumbing the white sticker in the right frame, I stated, "I guess somebody designed them all right."

"And I can see much better with them on than when they're off."

"I'm sure you can,"

"How do I look, Vince?" he asked as he placed the glasses carefully on his head.

"Great, Burt, very cool looking."

He nodded agreeably and strolled off in a clockwise direction with a big grin on his face. Burt wears his new sunglasses with regularity while he walks clockwise around the mall. He is so proud of those glasses. One day I asked Burt, "What is that string doing around your finger?"

"I tied this on this morning," he replied, "to remind me of something."

"Remind you of what? I asked.

"It's quite simple," he said, holding up his finger. "You see that knot? That's to prevent my forgetting. It's there…a forget-me-knot. A forget-me-not is a flower. It was a box of flour I am supposed to bring home."

"Ingenious," I cried in sheer admiration.

On one occasion, he said, "Hi, I'm here," as he passed me, walking in the wrong direction, of course. I was glad to hear he knew where he was.

Bouncing Burt is an affable fellow who brings a ray of sunshine into a rather gloomy environment.

Much Ado About Nothing

Decked out in white chino pants, a blue shirt, and white loafers is Sal. His neatly trimmed mustache accents his rather uninteresting facial features. He is a head shorter than me, is given to a paunch, and is slightly bald with a fringe of gray that matches his mustache. The blousy, open shirt with dangling chains around his neck reminds me of a character in a 1950s Fellini Italian movie.

Sal positions himself outside the hair salon every day—all day. I thought he might be the owner of the salon and was counting the number of customers who entered.

I discovered he doesn't own the salon, and no one knows why he hangs there all day. He appears to be harmless, apathetic, and unmotivated.

Occasionally he does speak to some mall busters, but not to me. Maybe I look too focused or direct, and he seems to have great difficulty looking anybody directly in the eyes, so I don't take his reticence personally.

Sal walks clockwise around the mall, carrying a coffee cup. He is most assuredly one of the "crazies." One day I asked him what he was doing at the hair salon. He said, "This is the best place to look at women."

All Dolled Up and Nowhere to Go

Olive is a prissy, eccentric ol' gal in her mid-sixties. She roams the mall, seemingly without direction. So many of the "crazies" do this. She zigzags with no apparent route in mind, and of course, walks in a clockwise direction.

In her vague velvet eyes, there dwells a look of earnest and limpid sincerity. She is all bones and pale skin, and when she walks, her body is rounded over like a pliable piece of balsam wood. Before she begins her walk, she ambles around, stretches her body quite tall, and lifts on her toes with her hands above her head. This is her starting position.

Olive wears heels and a colorful frilly dress, and carries a large matching handbag that she carefully guards. On her head sits a huge hat that nearly covers her eyes. Her hair is probably tied up in a bun beneath that hat, but I don't dare ask.

She has bowed legs. Perhaps she was a dancer in her younger years or rode horses when she was young. She'd never get a job catching pigs in an alley. Olive seems preoccupied and lost. She never looks at anyone but focuses her stare straight ahead as she saunters from one side of the mall to the other. No, she is not inebriated or tipsy, but her short, abrupt steps indicate she is preoccupied with other matters. Her melancholy eyes peer through the crowd as she enters a gift store.

Perhaps she is planning to buy some "Salopian China" for a dinner party she is preparing for a close friend. I hope she remembers to purchase food for dinner.

Then she pigeon-toes her way into a big fluffy armchair, in which she drops and turns her toes in. She ritualistically closes her eyes and clasps her hands tightly in her lap, dearly holding on to her purchase. She sits still and appears to meditate.

I wonder if Olive replaces buttons when they fall from her coat, remembers to mail letters, or places books upside-down on shelves. Oh, Olive. Have you always been this fragile?

THE UNEXPECTED

I shall never forget Thursday, June 3, for as long as I live. The day began inauspiciously, but just about everything went wrong.

Rain-rain-rain! Pitiless, ceaseless rain! No such thing as putting a foot out of doors, unless of course, you are dedicated to the regime of walking. The rain continued to fall heavily, with the wind blowing like a blustery nor'easter. I decided that even if it rained buckets—that made no difference. I figured there would be fewer walkers coming out in a torrential rainstorm. Just think, I can have the entire mall to myself!

As I got out of my car and ran a few hundred feet to the mall entrance, I realized I was soaked. Alas, no place to change into dry clothes, plus I didn't have the luxury of bringing extra clothes with me.

The workers were furiously mopping the floors with vigor as mall busters entered.

I turned to begin my routine counterclockwise walk around the mall when I noticed a picture of Albert Einstein on the wall. I was shocked to see a photo of him with his tongue sticking out! Under no circumstances can I understand why anyone would attempt to caricature and misrepresent a famous person's image for personal gain or to attract attention to a product. Using images of George Washington, Abraham Lincoln, and Teddy Roosevelt, among others, is not a practice that I find tasteful or amusing.

Suddenly, precisely at 8:45 a.m., a shrill squeal pierced the air as an alarm was tripped in one of the clothing stores. Certainly, the sounding of the shrill alarm would produce an immediate reaction in those who heard it. It was not the kind of thing anyone could listen to with complete indifference. The pitch was too overwhelming for that. The walkers were caught unaware, and all the "crazies" stopped to gawk as Rocco, the mall security guard, investigated the problem.

Rocco and the workers, who were attempting to locate the problem, were followed intently by the "crazies," who asked many questions about the noise. They were particularly concerned about whether it would happen again. When the unexpected happens, most people react according to their frame of mind, but "crazies" really can't handle unexpected and unforeseen events very well.

The "crazies" were getting quite restless and impatient. The alarm caused a considerable stir, so much so that Olive looked even more bewildered and lost than usual. This type of unexpected interruption in her daily routine throws her for a loop.

Bouncing Burt, who was standing around in a very casual way, suddenly began to frantically jump up and down to see above everybody's shoulders. Presumably, he believed that the higher elevation would enable him to assess the problem better than anyone else.

The sane walkers just rubbernecked the situation in passing as they kept walking in a counterclockwise motion. This must have been a troubling event for the "crazies." The most surprising part of the whole thing to me was that I did not feel in the least alarmed.

Now the "crazies" collective curiosity was at a fever pitch. They stared and looked intently into the store. At one point, the mall guard and four workers interlocked their arms, forming a human chain, which held back the eager and impatient "crazies."

"Don't be afraid," blurted out Rocco, with a self-satisfied air. "There's no reason to worry. No fire or explosions will happen."

"But egad," said Bouncing Burt, rubbing his hands together. "We might all die!"

"No way!" reassured Rocco in his explosive, gritty bass voice. "Look and see how calm I am."

The "crazies" slowly began to calm down.

I decided to continue walking in a counterclockwise direction, going about my day. Thankfully, the sirens and the eccentricities of the "crazies" soon subsided.

By the way, in what direction do you walk around the mall?

7

GOURMET FOOD AND OTHER OUTLETS

THE HAIR SALON

Bruno is my hairstylist. Even though I don't have a lot of hair to work with, he does his best. He is endowed with a full mane of thick, jet-black hair. Am I envious? You bet I am, but I have learned to live with that.

Bruno speaks with a broken Italian accent and likes to tell funny stories.

"Do you know why the Payless Store always needs workers?" he asked.

"No why?" I replied.

"If they changed their name from "Payless" to "Pay more" they would attract more people."

He smacked his thigh with his right hand and laughed heartily while I politely grinned. He had a pair of scissors in his left hand, and I wasn't about to tell him that the joke wasn't funny.

The next time I visited Bruno, he said, "A man had a small dog."

"Spitz?"

"No, just barks!"

I thought he would fall to the floor laughing as he clapped his hands in youthful glee. People frequently react that way when they win the lottery.

Bruno likes opera (particularly Verdi and Puccini), and classical music. He also watches television while cutting my hair. I'm not sure what my hair will look like when he is done cutting it. Perhaps it all depends on the type of program he is watching at the time.

Speaking about television, unlike attending the movies, I can easily run to the refrigerator during every commercial and make a provolone and prosciutto sandwich or spread ricotta cheese on eight crackers and gobble them up. This I have been known to do within a 30-second time frame.

However, I find that television has also caused our attention spans to shrink. Anything longer than a 15-second commercial sound bite is difficult for us to focus on, let alone listening to a 35-minute symphony by Brahms or Beethoven.

A publicist friend recommends that in today's business world, one should produce a promotional video of no longer than one minute!

Sound bites! Cracker bites! Chips and dip! These have all become part of our lives without realizing our attention spans have been dwindling and shrinking to the size of a cracker.

Newsstand

Operated by a foreigner and located at one corner of the mall is a newsstand. Now understand there is nothing inherently wrong with foreigners. My grandparents were foreigners and adapted well to American customs while steadfastly preserving Italian culture and traditions.

My parents were told by their parents, "You're in America now, act like an American." Speak English, go to school, improve yourself, and work hard. This was the recurring message from my parent's generation.

The person who operates this newsstand doesn't talk a lot and seems disinterested in everything except taking my money for newspapers, gum, and other sundries.

One day I stopped to buy a newspaper, and I asked him, "What do you think of the Yankees?"

"So sorry, I do not follow politics," he replied.

He wasn't sophisticated enough to know about the Mets or Yankees. What a uniform and disconcerting answer. I was thrown off balance by his remark and his obvious apparent lack of interest in what is going on in the New York area. He wasn't even trying to relate to our culture or adequately enlighten himself to carry on a semi-intelligent discussion with regular folks. What a lack of good judgment on his part.

I like newsstand workers who can talk about the latest current events, whether they are baseball, the weather, or the stock market. They should at least have some understanding of American sports and American culture so they can converse with the average customer. After all, a conversation is a good practice that keeps customers coming back.

MOVIE THEATERS

A cluster of eight movie theaters is in the mall. On the occasion when I go see a movie with my wife, we watch the movie with only six or eight others in the theater. Oddly, the movie is usually highly rated by "the experts."

I don't care to see many movies anymore, even if it is cheaper on a Wednesday afternoon. I recently perused some of the titles being offered, *Knocked Up*, *Waitress*, *Hostel Part II*, and *Paris, je t'aime*. These are not exactly titles that draw my interest or my curiosity.

Often the acting amounts to nothing more than passionate, emotional promptings in front of a camera. So many special computerized effects dominate many of today's movies and distract the actors from showing any authentic or genuine, convincing emotion. Sleaze and self-indulgence are the messages that leave audiences cold and desensitized. I wonder who thinks up the stories that appear on the screen?

In the same way, I compare the more recent pop music recordings with all the overdubs, effects, melismatic rantings, and screaming by the vocalists to the more unadulterated, pure vocal artistry of Sarah Vaughan, Lena Horne, Ella Fitzgerald, and Billy Holiday. The contrast in the approaches to singing among the newer pop artists and the recognized traditional vocal artists is quite startling and unsettling.

I just learned that all six movie theatres were closed indefinitely at the end of this month. The owners cited their leases were up and that attendance is off. In addition, sales and rental of DVDs and downloading online provides one with alternatives to sitting in a gargantuan movie theater with only six other people attending.

MANNEQUINS

In passing the women's dress shops, I couldn't help but notice the expression, or lack thereof, on the female mannequins posing in the windows. I am glad they don't talk as did the photo machine. The expression on their faces appears to be joyless and somber. Why can't the mannequins have expressions that radiate contentment and joy? I wonder if the person who fashioned these mannequins feels depressed and miserable.

Would I care to speak with or to spend time with these mannequins if they were alive: Not on your life! If they were alive, they would no doubt walk the mall clockwise.

ETHNIC FOODS

If I lived as if I was still 18 years old, I would regularly eat chocolate cupcakes covered in thick white marshmallows, washed down with an orange soda, and I'd be shocked if I ever saw McNuggets on a chicken.

Most of the mall busters grab a bite to eat from the fast-food outlets or the deli. At the popular Deli-Bagel Shop, the scrumptious muffins are so large that they look at least three times the size of the muffins my wife bakes. All the pastries are enormous and sugary, tantalizing and tempting, but high in calories and sugar. One bagel contains approximately 400 calories without added cream cheese. That's why I walk.

The Italian eatery opens at 10 a.m., and I often miss this grand event. When I look at the cost of one slice of pizza, I am glad to go elsewhere to eat.

On a rainy Wednesday, I stopped at the pizza outlet and looked at the variety of pizzas in the glass-enclosed case.

"What do you want?" the worker asked.

"A slice of pizza, please," I replied.

"What do you want on it?"

"Cheese and tomatoes would be nice, thank you."

He gave me a disparaging look and mumbled something under his breath.

"A plain slice will be fine for me," I repeated.

"No pepperoni or sausage?" he inquired.

"Not for me, thanks."

"Do you want it heated?"

"Of course, doesn't everyone?" I added, "Does it cost more if you heat it?"

He gave me a nasty look, as though his very existence depended upon selling me a slice of pizza with something on it. Purchasing a plain slice of pizza is a rather difficult process.

He grumbled and placed the slice of pizza in the oven. About three minutes later, he took the slice of pizza out of the oven, slid it onto a paper plate (a real class act), and took my money.

I am always appalled when workers who serve food also handle money with the same hand. I can see the millions of tiny germs on the money just waiting to jump onto my slice of pizza.

When I asked for a receipt, I thought he would detonate. I snarled at him and asked again for a receipt. He reluctantly threw the receipt at me and again grumbled. He wasn't Italian, so I couldn't insult him in the manner to which I was accustomed. Lucky for both of us. I was contemplating throwing some alphabet soup in his direction, hoping that the alphabet would say something nasty to him. Instead, I walked away.

I have yet to see a worker in the Italian eatery that looks in any way Italian. However, it doesn't appear to bother most folks. I wonder if these same people would feel as comfortable ordering Asian food from an Italian or soul food from a Norwegian.

I walk past two Asian food venues as I jaunt my two miles walking in a counterclockwise direction. Every time I pass these two adjacent restaurants, two petite-looking Asian girls hold up a greasy-looking piece of meat impaled on a toothpick, smile, and say, "Taste very good, very good."

One day I summoned the nerve to ask, "What is that?" while she was dangling the piece of meat in front of me on a wooden toothpick.

"Teriyaki chicken with sesame seeds," she replied.

"How do you prepare it?" I inquired.

"Just fry them a long time," she replied.

"Sometimes with cheese, and we have it cold, too," she replied, decked out with a green apron and a little red hat.

I decided to pass on the sample and continued walking. I am convinced that eating fast food regularly will get a person to heaven quicker.

Card Store/ Mattress Store/ Hat Store

I seldom go to these stores. For the price of a greeting card, I can buy lunch at the local diner. As for the mattress store, I have never seen anyone leave or enter that store, and the manager is there without a friend in the world, along with his thoughts and the unused mattresses.

One thing I do like about the store is a squeezable bright red pillow displayed outside the store that says, "Squeeze Me!" Guess what? I do just that as I walk by. I'm so glad the pillow doesn't say, "Hello, my name is Leonardo."

I have never been a great admirer of hats. The hat store displays hundreds of sports caps in a variety of colors, brands, and sizes. I have often observed teenage boys who wear their sports caps backward on their heads with the visor in the rear. Why do they do this? Some say that the visor against the neck protects the neck from sunburn, but teens don't play or work in the sun. Teens are too busy on their computers, iPods, and cell phones to go out in the sun. They all look alike; hardly a token of individualism.

I remember the only time I wore my baseball cap backward was when I was catching up in a baseball game, and the face protector mask wouldn't go on unless I turned the cap around.

I wonder how a store that has to pay rent, utilities, worker's fees, insurance, and other expenses can sell enough hats to make a reasonable profit. Then there is the candle store, which sheds light all on its own.

PET STORE

About 7:30 a.m. on a damp Wednesday, some mysterious impulse caused me to rise and peer through the pet store window where about thirty dogs of all shapes and sizes were housed in small, metal, see-through cages.

As I stared through the window, a tiny black and white dog closest to the entrance began to yap, yap, and jump up and down in a frenzied fashion. He was no doubt excited to see me and under the assumption I would feed him or take him home with me. He was wrong on both counts.

I watched attentively as a young girl in a bright blue uniform approached each dog. She gently picked each up in her arms and then hugged and kissed them on the mouth. Yuk! She handled the puppies in an affectionate way while she cleaned their cage and refilled their gravity-system water bottles. I admired her fervent love of dogs, and no doubt, she will someday make a great veterinarian or mother.

For the next three days, the large white dog in the brown metal cage watched my every move. He barked incessantly and jumped up and down with anticipation.

"Buy me, take me, feed me," he snapped. The smell of dog dreams was everywhere as I passed by. If he were let loose, he would no doubt run clockwise around the mall.

ART GALLERY

I have always loved art that moves me. Art that makes me think about a life that is kinetic and evokes in me a passionate response.

The art gallery is a rather curious place with an assortment of prints to fit anyone's taste. There are prints of famous paintings along with some ordinary ones.

I notice in the display window, two prints; one that replicates popular culture and the other characterizing artistic achievement. These prints are displayed side-by-side like proverbial twins.

A print of Van Gogh's "Starry Night" is adjacent to a print of two NASCAR drivers holding cans of beer. What a juxtaposition of opposites! One is instantly gratifying and identifiable, while the other requires concentrated viewing, study, and reflection.

The NASCAR print emphasizes the popularity and personality of the performers rather than the characteristics of the work in the Van

Gogh print. A great work of art imprints itself in our lives and increases our taste for something better, while works of popular culture touch us where we are and leave us essentially unchanged—empty.

I was taught that art selects what is significant and suppresses the trivial. Today's television reality shows present just the opposite approach. Its inferior acting, trivial dialogue, laugh tracks, and promotion of attitudes of retribution and dishonest ways to win at all costs are most disturbing. I find these shows to be less an aspect of art and more entrenched in the instant gratification of popular culture.

Just as I am ready to leave the mall, a big guy with a mustache springs past me in a half-crouch feinting at the air with left and right jabs. He was grunting as he struck with the right and left jabs. He was mildly "crazy" but harmless.

I must be on my way. The "crazies" are heading my way, and I don't want to confront them. At the mall door, I turn to take a sad, fond look at them all, their clockwise motion making me a tad dizzy.

AS THE DOORS CLOSE

Is my life more exciting than the sixty minutes I spend every day walking at the mall? Definitely. I am so fortunate as to count the mall busters among my friends, but I'm thankful I don't walk clockwise!

Being a mall buster has opened my eyes to what "normal" really means.

The last time I saw the cast of characters was on Super-Duper Sale Day at J.C. Penney. All my "friends" were at J.C. Penney's door one hour ahead of time. The first two hundred people got an extra 50% off their purchase. They swooped in as the doors opened and were swallowed up by the material jungle. Never to be seen again!

Before I became a mall buster, I traveled a lot.

PART II

Globetrotting Counterclockwise

"Develop interest in life as you see it; in people, things, literature, music. The world is so rich, simply throbbing with rich treasures, beautiful souls, and interesting people.
Forget yourself."

- Henry Miller

8

Are We There Yet?

Traveling often involves a degree of uncertainty and risk, such as the fear of flying.

A few famous people exhibited fear, such as Julius Caesar. He conquered the world, but he was terrified of thunder. Peter the Great of Russia cried like a child when he had to cross bridges.

When our children were young, and we'd take a trip, they'd keep asking, "Are we there yet?" They didn't understand that the purpose was not just reaching the destination but enjoying the trip. I explained to them that life is like taking a trip and we should try to enjoy each moment along the way. There was no response. Those who make the end a goal often miss the enjoyable things of life, like personal relationships, family, and friends. If achieving goals is our barometer for feeling successful, then we are in for a roller-coaster life full of wide-ranging experiences and drastic mood changes.

The famous scientist, Albert Einstein, was traveling on a train and the conductor asked him for his ticket. Einstein reached into his coat pocket searching for his ticket. It was not in his coat. Perplexed, he next checked his travel pouch, his briefcase, and even his hat for the ticket…but alas, no ticket could be found.

"That's okay, Mr. Einstein," the conductor exclaimed. "I know who you are, and don't you worry about it."

The conductor then went on to collect tickets from the other passengers. On his return, he saw Einstein crawling on the floor on his hands and knees in a panic.

"Don't worry, Mr. Einstein, you don't need a ticket. I know who you arc," the conductor reassured.

Einstein replied, "I know who I am also, but I must find my ticket so I will know where I'm going!"

General Douglas MacArthur said, "Nobody grows old by merely living for many years. People grow old by deserting their ideals. You are as young as your faith, as old as your doubt, as young as your self-confidence, as old as your fear, as young as your hope, as old as your despair."

First, let me share with you some experiences I had traveling the globe. We have been fortunate to travel to China, Spain, Portugal, Morocco, Israel, Egypt, Hong Kong, Mainland China, and Canada. Nova Scotia, and of course, throughout the United States, including Hawaii.

I will, of course, approach my travels moving in a counterclockwise direction beginning in the Orient. Life is a daring adventure.

THIS IS SHOW BIZ!

Norma and I have been blessed with three wonderful children: Stephen, Regina, and Matthew. Matthew is the youngest, and the show biz bug caught hold of him at a very early age. After viewing the movie, *The*

Wizard of Oz and almost memorizing the entire movie, he began to produce his puppet shows at age six.

Each night after dinner, Matt would inform us that the show would begin in 10 minutes. He couldn't tell the time yet, but he picked up the phrase from his mother when she would announce when dinner is ready. We ambled into our large living room on 6 Gabriel Drive in the town of Cortlandt in New York (about an hour north of New York City), and as we entered, we received a handbill for the show from Matt. He was the usher and of course, he couldn't spell or write, so he scribbled something on each handbill.

Matt would then announce the title of the production, switch on the spotlights (two lamps near him), begin the music from a cassette player, and then provide us with a humorous and creative show. We would laugh and applaud throughout the production.

Our prediction that Matt would make a life in show business came true many years later when he went to college and majored in theatre at SUNY New Paltz, New York.

After his graduation, he moved to New York City, worked as a waiter in upscale restaurants in New York City, and took acting classes in the Meisner technique of acting.

He acted in numerous shows and directed as well. Later, he began teaching the Meisner technique and opened an acting studio on 36th street in NYC. Matt has recently opened another acting studio in Miami. He was also nominated for a Tony Award in 2015.

UP, UP AND AWAY!

"Two of the greatest gifts we can
give our children are roots and wings."
- Hooding Carter.

It was the summer of 1984, and my family and I were on an airplane after I was asked to record music in Hong Kong. This was the first flight for my three children. After a 23-hour flight, landing in Japan, we were now eating food much different from the food prepared by my wife. Japan offered a distinct change in our diet even before we arrived in Hong Kong. We weren't too sure what we were eating or what was ahead.

9

Welcome to Hong Kong

We were greeted at the airport by a member of Youth with a Mission (YWAM) missionary team. We then stuffed ourselves into a taxi and journeyed to the missionary base on Borret Road on Hong Kong Island. During the taxi ride, my daughter Regina gasped and yelled, "We're all going to be killed. The driver is on the wrong side of the road!"

Our host chuckled and explained that driving in Hong Kong was just like driving in England.

While in Hong Kong, we stayed with missionary friends at a YWAM facility that was formerly the military hospital used by the

United States in WW II. The hospital was featured in the film, *Love Is a Many-Splendored Thing* with William Holden and Jennifer Jones. We recognized the hospital building with the panoramic view of Hong Kong Harbor years later when we saw a rerun of the movie.

Our first night in Hong Kong found me lying in bed, savoring all the sights we had seen that day. I was staring at the ceiling, and I noticed a dark spot about six inches long. Suddenly the spot moved! I was a bit unnerved—realizing it was a giant cockroach. I got out of bed, hastily grabbed a large broom from the hall, and attacked the monster. With all my gusto, I finally subdued the roach. Maybe David felt that way when he slew Goliath. Victory over the roach was mine, and I savored the moment. My wife asked what I was doing running around the room waving a broom. After I explained my calculated approach and plan of attack, she was less than impressed that I had saved her from this horrible man-eating monster!

On our second day, I awoke at 6 a.m. anticipating what new experiences we would encounter that day. After suffering through a cold shower, we had breakfast with over 200 YWAM missionaries. We walked down Borret Road to catch the Star Ferry to mainland Hong Kong. The Star Ferry cost ten cents and only five cents if you wished to ride the lower deck. Most of the passengers were Chinese, smartly dressed, polite, and kept to themselves. This was so unlike the subways in New York City.

As we walked toward the Star Ferry, I spotted a tall, lean Chinese rickshaw driver. I have always been curious about rickshaws after watching Charlie Chan movies as a young boy. Fascinated by this cultural phenomenon, I quickly raised my 35-millimeter camera and snapped his picture. He glared at me as I took his photo. He began shouting at me, "Hey, you," and chased me around the ferry terminal. I was naturally dumbfounded and eluded him by quickly ducking into the nearest toilet facility. It was all happening so fast. My family laughed at the unexpected spectacle as several hundred onlookers watched with curiosity. I later found out that rickshaw drivers expect to be paid for taking their pictures. Who knew? Two dollars would have calmed the situation considerably. Within my first days in Hong Kong, I suddenly became an ugly American with a Chinese man chasing me.

PERILOUS JOURNEY

The day started like any other, but my trouble began one evening when we were invited to view a multimedia presentation on Lamma Island. I politely asked my host where this island was located, and he told me it was about 45 minutes across from Hong Kong in the middle of the South China Sea. We decided the adventure of the trip would be worth the effort. Ten students from YWAM who lived in Hong Kong accompanied us and were our guides.

It was a gray and overcast 6 p.m. when we boarded a hydrofoil to Lamma Island. We landed in the dark, and I led the group of ten young folks up the shore to the dusty road about 50 yards away. Lamma Island was littered with wet straw that had been lying there for a long time. In one corner was a stagnant pool of water surrounding an island of dark muck. There were several featherless chickens crowded together under a cart. Near the cart was a dozing cow chewing the cud and standing patiently while a small brown dog uttered something now and then between a bark and a yelp.

Most folks lived in barrios or shanties on Lamma Island. Large rats were everywhere. No windows had screens. There was no running water and limited electricity. It was a stifling 95 degrees with high humidity. None of the natives spoke English. Hardly a place to be while on vacation!

Following the multimedia production, the local pastor invited us to his home for dessert and tea. He and his wife spoke English, and their home had modern conveniences like running water and toilets.

A young boy excitedly darted into the room and screamed something in Chinese. He was breathing heavily, and there was a look of panic on his face. His words came rushing out like a cascade of crazy excited sentences, and he didn't stop until he ran out of breath.

Something was wrong. I asked my host what he said. He said that we missed the last hydrofoil for mainland Hong Kong. I was somewhat staggered at the remark. I swallowed hard and gasped with apprehension, trying to digest what had just happened. We had to act quickly. The thought of having to stay overnight on Lamma Island was not an inviting one.

My daughter, Regina, gasped and covered her mouth.

"I have a bad feeling about this," my son, Steve, said.

"I feel sick," remarked a YWAMer as her knees were shaking.

I tried to calm everybody as sweat trickled down my neck and under my shirt collar.

This prompted a reply from our host as he anxiously announced the one sure route out of this quandary. "You *must* take a Chinese fishing junk back to the mainland immediately.

I could not believe what I was hearing. There was an uneasy silence, as feelings of nervousness and worry quickly filled the room. I was seriously debating in my mind whether this could be the end of my missionary career. I finally caught my breath enough to mutter, "What does this mean for us?"

The thought of smelly fish and water-laden wood overwhelmed me. In the face of an inexplicable and uncharted problem, we cautiously approached the dock. Our flashlights were burning brightly, and we were astounded to see a Chinese fishing junk anchored about thirty feet from shore. We gasped in unison.

An old bent-over, wrinkled-face Chinese junk captain with several missing teeth smiled at us. He motioned for us to come aboard, but what we saw next terrified us even more. An unsteady, warped narrow wooden plank extended about 30 feet from the dock to the Chinese junk.

"Oh, my God," screamed Shirley as she looked at the board. "We're all gonna die!"

The captain beckoned us to walk the plank to the boat. Perspiration rolled down my face as I felt the blood boiling in my veins and my stomach doing flip-flops. I was as close to being sick. I don't even like to walk on an uneven sidewalk, let alone a narrow strip of warped wood.

We carefully pondered and discussed his invitation for a while before deciding to inch our way from the shore to the junk. A cold realization finally hit me; being the oldest and not wanting to appear afraid, I offered to lead everyone from the shore to the junk. "We can do it!" I stammered. I nodded to the captain. He gave a sympathetic murmur. You could smell the salt air and hear the waves pounding against the old wooden junk.

Terror struck me as I swallowed several times. I smiled briefly and told everyone not to look down. Once perched on the plank, we held each other's hands and cautiously took one step at a time toward the junk on my verbal count. I loudly counted "one," and we all moved one step to our left on the plank. What if it wouldn't hold us? It took about twenty precarious minutes to complete our course and board the junk. I was thinking, "My God, we could have fallen into the South China Sea and swept away forever without anyone knowing we were missing."

A lovely evening turned unexpectedly into a night of terror and an adrenalin rush.

After a long wait, we sensed a shimmer of motion as the boat bobbed away from the pier. As the bright lights of Hong Kong Island flickered ahead of us in the distance, a sense of exhilaration filled our bodies and spirits. We made our trip back to mainland Hong Kong in a little over two hours. No power on Earth could get me to go back to Lamma Island!

TAXI RIDE

It was mid-December, and the temperature was in the high sixties. We just finished recording in the studios, and I was sitting in a taxi with Daryl Ching, a Chinese man born in Los Angeles and now living in Hong Kong at the YWAM base.

I was discussing with Daryl that I find it amusing how foreigners interpret the English language. For example, I saw a sign posted in a Hong Kong tailor shop that read, "Ladies may have a fit upstairs."

Please allow me to digress a bit. A few weeks earlier, when traveling with Gary Stephens, a friend who lived in Hong Kong, we took a taxi from the Star Ferry Terminal to the YWAM base on Borret Road.

I heard Gary say to the Chinese taxi driver *Bo-ro-do,* using three distinct pitches (high, medium, and low). This meant Borret Road in Chinese.

Back to my taxi ride with Daryl Ching. Daryl was attempting to tell the Chinese taxi driver how to get to Borret Road in Chinese. The taxi driver just shrugged his shoulders and looked puzzled each time Daryl tried. At the moment, Daryl was less concerned about getting home than he was about his apparent inability to communicate with the Chinese driver.

I chirped in *Bo-ro-do* using the three pitches (high, medium, and low) I heard my friend Gary use a few days earlier. The taxi driver said, "Okay," smiled, and took off for Borret Road. Daryl and I looked at each other in amazement, and I could scarcely keep from laughing out loud.

It seems as though the brash New Yorker outdid the Chinese man in Hong Kong! Again, my musical ability and ear for pitches bailed me out of a tense situation.

Night Market

Our friends took us to a night market in the old Chinese Kowloon section of Hong Kong. We were warned that under no circumstances should we eat anything sold at the market. I asked if we could eat anything offered for free. The answer was definitely, "No." The air was dense with the aroma of exotic spices. We observed the gambling in smoke-filled archives, seedy-looking opium dens, snake shops, and people eating birds and turtles and other far-out things.

We were quite amused to see two men squatting on the ground. One man was examining and filling the other man's teeth. He was no doubt the Night Market resident dentist. Even if I were in severe excruciating pain, I would wait until I got back to the States to see my dentist.

Suddenly I saw a man selling pineapple slices, which looked appetizing. After all, what's wrong with eating fresh pineapple? Foolishly forgetting what my friends said about not eating the food, I motioned to the vendor with one finger that I wanted a slice of pineapple. I paid him 25 cents. He promptly swiped the slice of pineapple through a tub of murky brown water and then handed it to me with a big smile on his face. One who is unversed in such matters can have no notion of the many things that can happen to a slice of pineapple, let alone pineapple dipped in muddy water. I quickly "deep-sixed" the pineapple slice into the nearest trash heap. The moral of the story: "Always listen to your friends, especially if they live in Hong Kong."

Nightclubs

Before arriving, I wondered what a nightclub in China was like. It was Saturday evening; I had just finished recording in the studios at 6 p.m. Gary Stephens and his family invited us to attend a show at a nightclub in downtown Hong Kong. In the United States, a nightclub would be considered full with 200-300 customers. In Hong Kong, things are a bit different. A 2000-person audience is not uncommon. The music was jazz and pop performed by some of the musicians I used earlier in the recording sessions. It was a spectacular show.

We sat at a table in the middle of the room, and I wanted to see who was playing. I forgot to bring my glasses. I repeatedly borrowed my wife's glasses, looked at the band, and handed them back to her. I wasn't sure why the Chinese folks around us began to laugh and snicker. I asked Gary why they were laughing. He said they were amused that a husband and wife share one pair of glasses. They thought we were too poor to afford two pairs of eyeglasses. We all had a great laugh.

Miniature Sumo

On one of our flights to Hong Kong, a young Asian boy of around seven or eight years of age, built like a young sumo wrestler, continued to run up and down the aisle. He made a disgusting noise by placing his hand under his armpit as he pumped his arm up and down. I found this most disturbing, especially since I was trying to sleep during the long 23-hour flight. I suddenly reached out, grabbed him as he ran by, and said in a firm voice, "Look, I own this plane, and I want you to sit down now!"

He stared at me long and hard with wide eyes and slowly retreated to his seat. A few hours later, he got up, walked toward the bathroom, and sheepishly eyeballed me as he ambled by. My schoolteacher persona worked.

Years ago, a similar occurrence happened in a movie theatre in the States when I took my three children to a movie. At the start of the film, children began running up and down the aisle, laughing and creating a commotion. I had had enough! I stood up in the theatre and shouted, "I came here to see a movie, I paid my money, and I want all of you to sit down and be quiet."

They all sat down, and their parents applauded my remarks.

LET MY WORKER GO!

During one of my recording sessions, while working with 24 string players from the Hong Kong Philharmonic Orchestra, we suddenly heard a loud banging sound coming from outside the studio. I immediately stopped the musicians, waited, and then continued to record. Again, the banging sound happened. I asked my assistant to go outside and investigate where the sound was coming from. He left and returned to inform me that it was a Chinese worker on a bamboo scaffold repairing a broken pipe on the exterior of the building.

I asked him to go back and ask the worker how much he was being paid for that day. My assistant returned to tell me, "He makes $15 for the day." I handed him the $15 and told him to pay the worker and send him home. We finished the six-hour session without further incident

10

Mainland China

"Travel and change of place impart new vigor to the mind."
- Seneca

In April 2000, I was fortunate to have been asked to accompany 360 artists, writers, and musicians on a cultural exchange program to mainland China. The International Festival of the Arts was an event I will never forget.

Thousands of people attended opening night at the theatre in Kunming. I was conducting the Kunming Symphony Orchestra and a choir from Toronto in a medley of Broadway songs for the vocalist, Mary Mancini. The response and prolonged applause were overwhelming. The next morning, I awoke and saw myself conducting the orchestra on Chinese National Television. A milestone achievement. In China, I was a celebrity!

As part of the cultural exchange program, we 360 artists worked with the Chinese as we taught, demonstrated our skills, and performed our art.

A string quartet from England was asked to go to lunch with some professors at the Chinese University following a performance. When they returned to the hotel, they told us what the Chinese ordered for appetizers—live maggots and bumblebees!

I asked what they did about it. They said they had to eat some of each so as not to embarrass their hosts. The Chinese consider maggots and bumblebees to be a delicacy. I'm not sure I wouldn't suddenly contract a sudden illness, shortness of breath, and faint. That would have been better than eating live maggots and bumblebees.

Twelve of us were invited for dinner at the home of the Minister of Culture in Kunming. We were transported by limousine and arrived in style. After the dreadful experience of members of the string quartet, I wasn't too anxious to attend the dinner. However, my deepest fears were short-lived. They served thinly sliced water buffalo and other items that I thankfully recognized.

I was impressed by the number of times the Chinese government officials offered toasts, quickly drinking Chinese white rice wine in small silver cups. A translator was seated at each table so we could understand what was being said. Each of us had a chance to stand and toast the Chinese and say a few words. This time I was careful not to use American colloquial slang that could easily be misinterpreted.

While rehearsing the Kunming Symphony Orchestra with vocalist Mary Mancini, I was impressed with the decorum and professionalism of the orchestra members. During the twenty-minute breaks in rehearsal, some of the orchestra members approached the podium to study my music scores. The Chinese are hungry to learn about Western music and Western ways.

LIQUID GOLD

During the 20-minute concert intermission, the performers went outside. Also, about 300 Chinese students were performing that evening. They were eating a meal consisting of garoupa fish and white rice while squatting on the ground. I reached into my pocket and pulled out a sheet of paper logo stickers I purchased from a Dollar Store in the States.

Suddenly, a stream of children burst out of the doors and into the courtyard. They surrounded me like they had taken a prisoner. They were jumping up and down with excitement, laughing and pointing to my stickers. The hordes of Chinese students mobbed me, reaching for the stickers, and all talking at once. It happened so quickly. They came toward me in frenzy and grasped for a sticker. The throng was so thick that I yelled to vocalist Mary Mancini to help me as I quickly threw her three or four sheets of stickers. The colorful stickers adroitly said things like: "Wow," "I Love New York," "Pow," "I'm the Best," "Wonderful," "Shazam," "You're the Greatest," and other motivational expressions. Despite the onslaught, we began to place one sticker on each student's uniform. I was somewhat surprised to see even the adult musicians in the orchestra wanted a sticker.

A few days before the opening concert, we were interviewed by two prestigious young Chinese women who were anchors for the national Chinese television station in Kunming. The next day following the concert, we were walking along the breezy and bustling streets looking for a place to eat lunch. To our amazement, the same two television anchors recognized us. Frantically they waved to us, and we made our way over to them. Of all the things they could have said to us, what they said surprised us the most.

"Do you have any more stickers?" they asked as they extended their hands toward me.

I was stunned. I reached into my coat and pulled out four stickers, the last four I had, and handed them to the young women. They were as happy as little schoolgirls. I suddenly realized that I had brought liquid gold to the Chinese in the form of paper stickers.

In a culture where drab colors, bicycles, poor people, and joyless faces prevail, simple things like Dollar Store stickers have real value.

Later in the trip, I was asked to present a workshop on Musical Theatre for students at the Chinese University in Kunming. The theatre was packed with over 500 eager Chinese music students. Vocal artist Mary Mancini and her husband-pianist Mario Tacca assisted with the workshop.

Working with an interpreter is usually difficult, and sometimes the translations of English words can get confusing.

A Chinese professor of music introduced me. I smiled and immediately said, "I am tickled to death to be here."

The interpreter gave me a blank stare and asked, "What do I do with that?"

"Just say it like I said it," I responded.

And so she did. Immediately snickers and chuckles emanated from the crowd of Chinese students.

At the end of the lecture, a friend who spoke both fluent Chinese and English approached me. "Do you know how your introductory statement was translated?" he asked.

"No, not quite," I said.

"Well, it came out. 'I'm itching and scratching and about to die.'"

It's no wonder the Chinese students reacted the way they did.

I was asked to present a workshop on Jazz Improvisation, working with a fine jazz septet from Austria. However, the Chinese officials at the Chinese University didn't want this workshop presented at the university. I surmised that the freedom displayed in jazz improvisation was a bit threatening to their control over the masses. Therefore, they moved the workshop to a nightclub in downtown Kunming. The students who attended were excited to be there. The innocence and hunger to learn among the Chinese seems refreshing. They have little in material possessions but offer much through their culture

11

ARRIVEDERCI ROMA

"Traveling is almost like talking with men of other centuries."
- Rene Descartes

With an ocean protecting me from the rickshaw driver's wrath and having to walk a wooden plank from Llama Island, the following year, my wife and I ventured to sunny Italy, the land of my ancestors. For years, I cherished the idea of going on this trip.

The land of my family ancestry is shaped like a boot. It is noted for its plentiful food and wine, extraordinary art masterpieces, tomato gardens, warm weather, and friendly people.

It was July 2nd when we landed in Rome with a tour group of about 40 and traveled by bus to the charming city of Sorrento. There, Norma and I met my brother Richard's friends who taught art and philosophy at the University of Naples. They graciously showed us the magnificent scenery in this delightful city. The spaciousness of the mountains and cliffs astounded us. We were treated to a sumptuous dinner in a trattoria-style restaurant that displayed verdant hanging gardens and white, lush waterfalls.

I can still smell the cappuccino, see the rose-colored paint on the walls, and hear the music played by the mandolins. My wife and I made sure to savor the moment.

While driving in our host's car, my curiosity awakened. I mentioned that I didn't see any stoplights in Sorrento.

"They put one up a few years ago," replied my host, "but no one paid any attention to it, so they took it down."

"That's so Italian," I said as we all roared with laughter.

Italian Opera

While in Rome, as we walked down a narrow side street, we heard a man singing an aria from a Verdi opera. We investigated further and noticed a taxi driver singing along with the music emanating from his car radio. He acted as if he were singing a solo on a two-hundred-foot stage at La Scala Opera House. His gestures were grand and simple; he moved about a great deal, never looking at anybody else. He was a handsome, healthy, cheerful-looking man in his early thirties. Perhaps he was a descendant of Enrico Caruso.

A taxi driver with such an intense passion, singing operatic arias on the street corner. This was unlike any taxi driver we ever met In New York City.

In Rome, people were constantly stopping me in the street to ask if I was from New York… probably because I was wearing an "I Love New York" T-shirt. I couldn't help but chuckle a little whenever I saw young Italians wearing T-shirts that read "Hard Rock Cafe," not even realizing what it meant.

My curiosity was aroused as I entered a large music store where all types of musical instruments were hanging on the walls. I saw instruments I never knew existed; those from the Renaissance were particularly fascinating.

The owner asked if I was a musician, and I told him I played the saxophone. When I explained that I owned and played a Mark VI Paris Selmer alto saxophone I purchased in 1964, his countenance brightened. He offered me a whopping $8,000 and said he would fly to the States to get the saxophone. I graciously declined, which caused his overconfident smile to droop with disappointment, as if I had just insulted his dead mother! I left thinking how fortunate I was to own such a classic saxophone.

We were with a tour group as we traveled around Italy. I always notice how actors in a movie always seem to find a parking space directly in front of their destination. However, parking a car in a foreign country is not as easy as Hollywood would lead us to believe (it can actually be a bit of a nightmare at times).

NOW I'M ITALIAN!

Before leaving for Italy, I purchased a book called *Speak Sentences in Italian*. I eagerly began learning as many sentences as I could. After a few days in Italy, I believed I was becoming fluent speaking Italian. After all, I grew up learning many Italian curse words, and I studied music in college, so I knew all the Italian musical terms.

I could now rattle off phrases in one breath, like: "Where is the hotel?" "How much does it cost?" "May I ask for directions?" "Can you help me?" and other practical everyday expressions.

I was so proud of my ability to speak Italian that I told my wife, "Norma, I bet they think I'm Italian, and I live in Italy."

With a little smirk and a bit of disbelief in her voice, she replied, "Sure, Vin. I bet they do."

So I stopped an Italian peddler selling ties and asked in my best Italian, "*Mi scusi Signor, quanta costa.*" Or, "Excuse me, sir, how much does this cost?"

He smiled and answered me in English! I was devastated and embarrassed. All the air in my balloon was let out. The Bible aptly states in Proverbs 16:18: "Pride goeth before destruction, and a haughty spirit before a fall." My wife laughed. What a jolt to my ego!

The Blind Leading the Blind

A majority of our tour counted on me to interpret road signs and other items of interest when our guide was preoccupied. (Hey, at least they recognized I was "fluent" in Italian!)

It all started one evening when about forty of us decided to attend a ballet in Rome. *Romeo and Juliet* by Profokiev was being performed in the beautiful Villa Borghese Park. It was a remarkable sight, with unique Tuscan cypress trees and the surrounding Roman countryside. I led the forty tourists by foot from the grand hotel to the park entrance. The crowd responded to the concert by being quiet. They were well-mannered and attentive during the performance. No one would dare speak or leave his or her seat during the performance.

The orchestra musicians wore tuxedos and played magnificently while the dancers splendidly rose to the occasion. During the performance, my wife remarked about the high shoes worn by the ballet dancers. "Don't you think their feet hurt standing on their toes in that way?"

"Maybe they should hire taller dancers," I replied.

As usual, my wife ignored my inane remark.

After the performance, I assembled the forty travelers for a stroll back to our hotel. We advanced to the main gate where we earlier entered the park. To our dismay, it was locked. Behind the gate stood two *carabinieri*, which are Italian policemen. In my best "Italian," I politely asked them to open the gate. *"Mi scusi, a che ora apriva il cancello?"*

"*Domani!* The gate won't be open again until tomorrow morning at nine," they answered in Italian.

I frantically responded in Italian, "What about all these people I am with?"

The two *carabinieri* began to hoot and howl.

Without thinking, I foolishly began to insult them in Italian. They laughed even louder. I hurled a few more choice, derogatory words in Italian with accompanying hand motions and walked back to my friends.

A bright idea then hit me… if cars are leaving the park, why don't we go out the same gate as the cars?

After we arrived safely back at our hotel, I explained what happened to our Italian guide. His face flushed of all color when he told me I could have been sent to jail for insulting police officers. He was so upset, he had to sit down. And I thought the rickshaw driver and walking the plank in Hong Kong was bad. This could have been a catastrophe. I will never know for sure what might have happened that night, but what I do know I didn't speak to any Italian policemen for the remainder of our trip.

We next ventured to Florence, which has to be one of the world's most stunning cities. While visiting a museum, I noticed some visitors being shown around by a museum guide. In the art gallery, certain masterpieces were beyond price, possessions of eternal beauty and unquestionable genius. Works by artists such as Rembrandt, Degas, Monet, Picasso, and others dominated our attention.

At the end of the tour, one visitor remarked, "Well, I don't think much of these old pictures."

The guide answered quietly, "I would remind you that these pictures are no longer on trial, but those who look at them are."

A marvelous response to someone who has done his best to show his pitiable blindness and obvious ignorance.

IT'S NOT BOGART!

The next year, Norma and I traveled with another tour group to sunny Spain and Portugal. We had the opportunity to visit Morocco off the coast of Africa. I've often wondered what Morocco was like. Now that I know, I wish I hadn't.

Remembering the 1942 movie *Casablanca* with Humphrey Bogart, we decided to go. Maybe someone would be playing the fashionable song, "As Time Goes By" from the movie.

To our astonishment, all the taxi drivers drove Mercedes Benz cars. We also saw flute-playing Arab snake charmers with cobras dancing in front of them and merchants selling all types of exotic stuff we weren't interested in buying.

Outside the huge tent where we ate lunch, we were treated to music played by an Arab band, playing on some musical instruments I had never seen or heard before. It was both strange and fascinating at the same time. Following a ten-minute appearance by two belly dancers, we happily ventured outside the tent to inspect the surrounding area.

Immediately my eyes focused on a huge camel and its owner. I didn't care about taking a ride on a camel, but I wanted my wife to take a picture of me sitting on top of the camel while he was lying on the ground.

I asked the camel owner if my wife could take a picture of me sitting on the camel. I told him that I did not want to ride the camel. He nodded agreeably and smiled profusely. I emphatically restated my request three times to make sure he got it right.

I assumed he understood me. I sat on the camel, which was lying quietly on the ground. As soon as I sat on the camel, the owner snapped his fingers, the camel stood up, rose to his full height (with me nearly falling to the ground on my face), and for the next five minutes, I rode around the tent area atop this tall and smelly animal. My wife was quite amused. At the end of the ride, the owner smiled and held out his hand expecting to be paid. I tried every persuasive tactic I could think of not to pay, but I gave up in despair and paid him $25.

Later, while strolling the streets of this little town and looking for Claude Rains or Humphrey Bogart to show up, four adorable little children approached us. They smiled at us so sweetly and innocently. They asked if we wanted to take a picture with them. How could we refuse such delightful and charming children? They huddled up to us and smiled while a friend took a picture. The next thing I knew, they held out their little paws and screamed, "Money, money."

When we hesitated and did not reach for our wallets immediately, the delightful little angels became incorrigible and infuriated monsters. They began pulling at our coats and yelling, "Money, money." We finally gave them two dollars each just to get rid of them.

Next, we were ushered by our inept guide into a gigantic Oriental rug store. The salesperson who approached us said, "Allah will bless me with a sale today, and *you* are the sale."

I replied that if Allah told him about us, he was mistaken because we certainly weren't in the mood to buy an Oriental rug. Such hustle and high-pressure tactics I had never seen. He almost demanded that I buy a rug from him. He said that Allah would not bless him if he did not sell me a rug *today*. He followed us around the store shouting in a foreign language. We quickly departed based on our misgivings of this unrelenting, unpleasant fellow.

We were relieved to leave this corner of the world.

When we returned to Spain, we felt that we required a shower to get rid of the stench of opportunism, avarice, and self-indulgence that might be lingering on our bodies.

I quickly added Casablanca to my list of places I'll never return to. So far, Llama Island and Casablanca were evenly tied for first place.

12

Let My People Go!

On March 19, 2007, twenty-one of us journeyed to Israel and Egypt for a 10-day tour. As we passed from Israel to Egypt, I noticed that the Egyptian customs officers seemed bewildered and confused. Our luggage was thrown around like bed pillows, and it took almost twenty minutes to haul our luggage to the inspection point.

I was tempted to comment on the apparent lack of order and decorum but decided I did not want to wind up in an Egyptian jail. Therefore, I opted to overlook the situation and kept my mouth shut. Believe me, this took willpower.

Our perky Egyptian guide Shaquilla told us she was looking for a husband and that Egyptians thrive on chaos and confusion. After spending three days in Egypt, I believed her on both counts.

Mount Sinai

Our first night was spent at the foot of Mount Sinai, where Moses received the Ten Commandments from God. It was a chilly evening. Our guide inquired as to who would like to climb to the summit of Mount Sinai (over 4,200 feet) to see the sunrise. Eight brave souls volunteered from our group. My wife and I were not among them. I figured if I was shivering at the foot of the mountain with my jacket on, I could wind up as a permanent ice statue at the top.

As for the eight volunteers, they were awoken at 1:30 a.m. and given coffee or tea in the so-called cafeteria at 1:50 a.m. At 2 a.m., they traveled by camel with a Bedouin guide leading them with a flashlight along a narrow mountain path. This lasted for one and a half hours. The camels could go no further due to the steep terrain and rocky slopes. Everybody dismounted and walked another one and half hours to the summit. After spending approximately fifteen minutes at the top of Mount Sinai watching the sunrise, they reversed course and traveled another agonizing three hours down the mountain. They arrived at the bus around 8:30 a.m. A tired, bedraggled, motley crew they were. They slept on the bus for the six-hour ride back to Cairo.

Chaos Reigns

Our visit to the pyramids and the Great Sphinx gave me a chance to see where the famous Sahara Desert begins. The sphinx had its nose clipped, and I asked our guide how it happened.

"Oh, Napoleon's soldiers used it for target practice," she replied, "and so did Hitler's men during World War II."

I nodded as though I believed it. There was only one mode of access to the pyramid. When asked if I wanted to go inside the pyramid, I asked what I had to do.

"Pay $15 and crawl 150 feet through a small tunnel on your hands and knees—and oh yes, there's hardly any air in there."

Unless someone tied a rope around my feet and pulled me out quickly when I screamed, I wasn't going to subject myself to that kind of torture. So, I declined the offer, as did all the other 20 people in our group.

More Chaos

The next morning at 8:30 a.m., our Egyptian guide informed us that she attended a rock concert in front of the Pyramids last evening. She brought her 16-year-old daughter to see a young American rock star.

She told us the concert was supposed to begin at 7:30 p.m., but it began at 11 p.m. and finished at midnight. It seems that there were no traffic police to direct the cars, no parking area, no attendants, no lights along the roads, and no place to sit once they arrived. Citing that it usually takes her about 35 minutes to drive to the pyramids, that evening, it took three hours due to the narrow roads and the vast number of cars.

After the concert, many people drove around the Sahara Desert, desperately trying to find their way out of the mess. She got home around 3 a.m. This was "chaos" at the maximum level.

Ups and Downs

While in Israel, I noticed that on Saturday, the Sabbath, there were the usual four elevators, but one was marked "Sabbath Elevator." This aroused my curiosity, and I investigated further. I found out that to the orthodox Jew, pushing a button on the Sabbath is considered work, and is therefore not allowed. Thus, the elevator marked "Sabbath Elevator" automatically stops at all 17 floors, both in the up and down direction. No one has to push a button! A creative approach to a complicated problem. I wondered how they entered their hotel room. Was sliding a plastic entrance key into the door slot considered work?

Having heard so much about the Wailing Wall, we were eager to visit it. Men are separated from the women at the Wailing Wall by a stone partition, and security is tight upon entering the gate. We got the opportunity to write prayers on tiny slips of paper and insert them between the rocks on the wall. A truly historic moment!

This is a very sacred place for the orthodox Jews, as they wail and bob their bodies up and down (davening) while offering up their prayers to God, covered by their prayer shawls. Our Jewish guide told us that on the Sabbath (Saturday), the orthodox Jews put on a big show with their wailing, crying, and exaggerated movements. Maybe God likes choreography.

How Much is That Bracelet in The Window?

Bargaining is one of my wife's specialties. She learned to do this from observing the Youth with a Mission students operate in Hong Kong markets.

In Egypt, I followed her as she walked into a jewelry store.

"How much is that silver bracelet?" my wife asked the shopkeeper in her usual sweet and gentle voice.

"Ah, a beautiful bracelet for a beautiful lady," he replied. "For the meager amount of $200, it will brighten up your day."

"It's too high," my wife answered. "One hundred dollars will brighten up my day even more."

"But I can't go that low for such a wonderfully made product…look," he said, trying to get her to hold it, but she refused. "How about $185?" he asked, quite possibly with a tear in his eye.

"Still too high," my wife said without flinching. "Ninety is my top offer."

"Madam," he pleaded. "You will make me cry, but I will lower the price to $175. How about that?

"I'm not interested," she said as she began to walk away.

"Okay. $115 is the best I can do," he muttered with a sad look.

"No—$90, and it's a cash sale… right now!"

"Okay, but you drive a hard bargain."

The owner looked at me as I shrugged my shoulders and smiled as though I had no control over my wife's haggling for the bracelet.

13

It's All a Misunderstanding

The word "Yankee" means different things to different people. In a *Wall Street Journal* article Robert W. Mayer writes, "To people in other parts of the world it simply means someone from the United States.; to people in the United States, it means someone from north of the Mason-Dixon Line; to us Northerners it means someone from New England; to New Englanders, it means someone from Vermont; to Vermonters, it means someone from the Green Mountains."

"One's destination is never a place, but a new way of seeing things." - Henry Miller

I expect folks to misunderstand or misinterpret English terms in foreign countries like China, Hong Kong, or Italy. However, my experience north of our border in Toronto, Canada, was a bit of a shocker.

A few years later, I was at the Toronto airport checking in at the gate. "Has anyone put anything in your baggage without your knowledge?" an airport employee asked.

"If it was without my knowledge, how would I know?" I replied.

"That's why we ask," he answered with a smile.

I caught this flight out of La Guardia Airport to Toronto because I was commissioned to write an original musical score for a dramatic dance piece called *Toymaker and Son*. I was to begin recording the next day with members of the Toronto Symphony.

"What do you do for a living?" I was asked at customs.

"I'm a conductor," I replied.

He asked me again, and I again responded, "I'm a conductor."

"Come with me," he said in a stern tone of voice.

Immediately, I was ushered into a large room with bare walls, a table, and one chair…where I was told to sit. Three uniformed guards were present, most likely to interrogate me. I could feel my heart beating like a tom-tom, and I began to grow restless. Did they think I was a foreign spy? A drug smuggler? A criminal of some sort? A member of the Russian KGB? I eventually found out that my initial response of "conductor" gave them the impression that I was a railroad conductor. They thought I might take jobs away from Canadians. It took me about 30 minutes to convince them that I was an orchestra conductor, patiently showing them my conducting baton, music scores, metronome, and other musical items I carry with me. During future visits to Toronto, I'll tell them I am a musician. Still, this unexpected inconvenience paled in comparison to the Chinese rickshaw driver, the Chinese fishing junk, and the Italian policemen.

Following one of the recording sessions with members of the Toronto Symphony Orchestra, I walked to lunch with one of the secretaries from the recording studio. She noticed the stoplight on the corner buzzes when it's safe to cross the street. She asked if I knew what the buzzer was for. I explained that it signals blind people when the light is red. She responded, "What on Earth are blind people doing driving?"

Both she and the Canadian customs officials must walk clockwise and should be considered "crazies."

14

DROPDOWN SIGN

"I have found out that there ain't no surer way to find out whether you like people or hate them than to travel with them."
- Mark Twain

During the late 1970s and 80s, our family of five traveled across the United States in our new, shining pop-up camper. While traveling for six weeks in close quarters, we had to retain our sense of humor. Our children learned and memorized the capitals and locations of most of the U.S. states we traveled through.

During one trip, we noticed a sign on a marquee outside a midwestern high school that read: "BA D CONCERT TONIGHT at 7:30." The letter "N: fell off. I often wonder if attendance at the concert fell off as well.

We stopped in Oklahoma City, Oklahoma; San Antonio, Texas; Hot Springs, Arkansas; and Baton Rouge, Louisiana to attend music conferences for high school band directors. We set up a display booth for the music we were selling at each conference site.

When the outdoor temperature hit a sweltering 105 degrees in San Antonio, Texas, our sneakers began to melt as we walked on the hot pavement. I looked inside my sneakers to see if there was a warranty!

We arrived in each city between 3 and 4 p.m., assembled our camper, and jumped into the campground pool. I was surprised to see we were the only ones swimming. I found out that most natives do not swim during the day due to the oppressive heat. Often the pool was as warm as bathtub water.

Next to the last night of our fourth trip across the USA, our camper top broke, and it could not be hoisted into proper position. We drove for miles looking for a motel, but since it was Saturday evening, we couldn't find anything with any vacancies. We drove to the nearest supermarket parking lot and attempted to sleep in the car. Our dispositions the next morning left a lot to be desired.

15

With a Banjo on My Knee

"The world is a book, and those who do not travel read only a page."
- St. Augustine

After teaching music at The King's College in Briarcliff Manor, New York for 16 years, the college began to feel the money squeeze from declining enrollment and low endowments. Talk began to circulate about its closing its doors forever.

I did not receive the news well. I discussed the matter with my wife for thirty seconds and promptly decided to apply to other colleges.

My fingers were flying, and my computer screen became a blur of activity as I carefully crafted hundreds of brilliant resumes and astute cover letters. I left no stone unturned in my quest to secure another college teaching position. I even considered returning to teaching public school music (for a total of ten seconds).

My phone bill increased in direct proportion to the decrease in my endurance level. The warm winds of summer rapidly approached, but answers to my letters of application seemed to be further and further away.

Remember the Dehumidifier

On July 8, Norma and I decided to accept an invitation from our friends, Dr. Charles Pierce and his wife, Eloise, to spend a few days with them at their cabin on a lake just outside Bangor, Maine. We arrived eager to see them while still a bit perplexed about my plans.

Charles is a quiet, unassuming person who always considers his words carefully before speaking. Eloise, on the other hand, is an impulsive, energetic, vivacious woman who is animated and fun-loving. She is continually busy and manages to swim five miles every day in their lake.

They appear to have a happy marriage, and Charles' approach to this can be summed up in this one episode that took place while we were with them. I call it "Remember the Dehumidifier."

It was a hot, dusty morning at the cabin, and we were enjoying an aromatic cup of imported coffee. Eloise had just completed her five-mile swim and was drying with a bright red towel. She babbled on about the cost of everything, government policies, and immigrants while the rest of us calmly nodded. Charles smiled and continued to pour more coffee into our bright orange cups. He asked me if I would accompany him to check his mail at his larger home in Bangor. I agreed, and we left in his blue mini-van.

It was a sweltering day at a sizzling 91 degrees with no apparent breeze blowing. As we entered the house, I noticed that dehumidifiers were running full blast, and the windows were wide open. I commented, "Charles, wouldn't it be better if the windows were closed with the dehumidifiers on?"

He calmly replied, "Eloise thinks they work better that way."

Not wishing to hurt Charles' feelings, I nodded as though I understood—but I didn't. I figured that if they were both happier with the dehumidifiers running full blast while the windows were open, why should I disagree and possibly shatter a good relationship?

WHAT'S NEXT?

Following our three days in Maine with Charles and Eloise, we drove back to our home outside Peekskill, New York. When the car stopped in our driveway, I bolted to our mailbox, anticipating numerous responses from the hundreds of applications sent.

Nothing. No responses. Not one person recognized my potential or realized my capabilities as a teacher.

I was in a state of mild shock and disbelief—realizing I must return to The King's College, which could mean the end of my illustrious teaching career.

As I entered my home, I heard a beeping sound and noticed a bright yellow light blinking on my answering machine. Upon pressing the lighted button, I heard an unfamiliar voice inform me that I was overqualified for the position listed at his university, but that a perfect job for me was available at Elizabeth City State University in Elizabeth City, North Carolina.

Having never heard of Elizabeth City, I promptly located it on our large colorful USA map. It was located approximately one hour south of Norfolk, Virginia on the northeastern tip of North Carolina near the Outer Banks.

When I arrived at The King's College the next day, I checked my answering machine and quickly realized the same message regarding the position at Elizabeth City State University was on it. Maybe this was a divine message that a door was opening for me to teach in North Carolina.

I promptly phoned the head of the music department at Elizabeth City State University. He liked what he heard and asked if I could come for an interview in two days. After a 10-second conversation with myself, I accepted the invitation, and two days later, I drove nine long hours to Elizabeth City. I checked into the local Holiday Inn and went on my first interview at the university.

Present were five members of the music department, the department chairman, and his secretary. I answered some questions, and they asked what I could offer the university. After reviewing the job description, I felt confident with the position offered: Director of Music Industry Studies. I would work with a professional recording engineer, teach all the music business courses, conduct the jazz ensemble, and direct the musicals. The university had just acquired a 24-track professional recording studio in which all sorts of music could be produced.

I was hired and hit the ground running as I began teaching three days later. I was fortunate to spend eleven exciting years building and developing the music industry program. We graduated many students who today are prominent figures in the music industry. And because of the students at Elizabeth City State University, I soon became well acquainted with hip-hop, rap, and gospel music.

You Want Me to Do What?

It was May 3rd, during my ninth-year teaching at Elizabeth City State University, when the assistant band director resigned and took a position at Duke University. Jeff Au was a good friend who helped me develop my music textbook and was a fine trumpet player and band director.

On August 1st, two days before the marching band camp was to begin, the band director hastily resigned to take a teaching position at a university in Mississippi. I felt the lateness of his resignation was very unprofessional and unfair to our students. I told him so, and my comments went over like a pork chop at a Bar Mitzvah! The students organized and ran the band camp and worked out the field show for the first football game.

No one in the music department had any experience with marching bands…except me! I had been a band director at Peekskill High School in New York for 17 years before leaving to teach at The King's College.

The Dean of the University summoned me to his office, asking if I could take on the extra duties of the marching band director until they could hire a replacement. I told them I would have to discuss this with my wife and would give them my answer the next day by noon.

I discussed this with my wife (much longer than 30 seconds), and we agreed I should take on the added responsibilities providing that the university agreed to the following:

1. This added responsibility would involve a lot more of my time.
2. The compensation should be appropriate for the level of responsibility and personal sacrifice of my time and social life.
3. The compensation earned should be applied to my retirement.
4. Provide an assistant to handle the scheduling and other mundane paperwork.

Realizing I was in a favorable negotiating position, and after a lengthy discussion, they agreed to my terms.

MAKE HASTE SLOWLY

My background as a marching band director was immersed in the "Big Ten" style of marching ala Ohio State or the University of Michigan. What I had now was a band that performed fancy dance routines to hip-hop and rock-funk music, and the female twirlers and dance team dressed and gyrating like Janet Jackson!

I remember what my dad told me many years before. "Make haste slowly, and don't try to change everything at first. Flow with it for a while, and then insert your ideas little by little." This was sound advice. I let the band do their type of marching maneuvers and helped them play more in tune without blasting all the time at full volume. I also tightened up their dance routines and field formations. After all, it had been more than 20 years since I last worked with a marching band and that was in the northeast at Peekskill High School.

On the Monday following our first half-time show, the Dean called me into his office and informed me that a department chairman had complained about me. I replied, "Already after only three days on the job?"

"Yes," he said. "He wanted to know why you were not wearing the white band uniform with the white hat and white gloves that the last directors always wore, and why you didn't conduct the Star-Spangled Banner at pre-game." I learned it was traditional for the band director to wear the white uniform with white gloves and conduct the national anthem while standing at the top of a platform ladder.

I feigned a little gasp and answered, "I wanted one of our top students to conduct with the white gloves and receive an ovation from the crowd. It is good for his self-image, and the experience is valuable for him. As for my not wearing the white band director's uniform, I will be glad to wear it when the football coach wears a football uniform!"

The Dean smiled and nodded in agreement.

"And please tell that department chairman to contain his remarks to his area of expertise and let me handle the band."

That was the first and last complaint I heard that year.

Gourmet Treats

Whenever the marching band participated in an away football game on Fridays, the business administration office supplied me with an envelope containing approximately $750 so I could pay for dinner for all band members following the football game.

The previous band director took the band to fast-food restaurants such as McDonald's or Hardees. I refuse to eat at these places, and I certainly would not encourage my students to do so.

During the week, usually on Monday, I would phone ahead to the local Golden Corral or steakhouse and informed them I was bringing 120 band members for dinner around 7 p.m. I asked for a break in the price plus free meals for the band directors, chaperones, and bus drivers.

The managers of the restaurants were most cooperative and eager to gain our business, my negotiating saved the university $100 or more, and the students ate plenty of food. My 6-foot-plus, massive tuba players would deposit enormous amounts of food on their plates, piled almost up to the lighting fixtures. When I informed them they could return for seconds or even third helpings, they looked at me and said, “Prof C, they might run out of food before we get a chance to go back.” I smiled as I listened to their logic and watched them scarf their food at about 50 miles per hour. Maybe they thought that I would take it away from them.

THE UNEXPECTED

We moved to Elizabeth City, North Carolina during the summer of 1993. Living in the South has its advantages: warm weather, lower housing costs, more reasonable restaurant and gasoline prices, friendly folks, and a more relaxed lifestyle.

One of the most conspicuous drawbacks to living in the South is hurricane season. One such storm struck Elizabeth City in 2002. We never experienced a major hurricane before. Upon hearing about the approaching hurricane, my wife and I decided to abandon our home and go to a local shelter. We were not brave enough to watch the pine trees in our yard bend in the wind and listen to hundreds of missile-pelting pinecones strike the windows in our home like missiles shot from a repeating canon. Despite the violent winds, our home survived with just a few shingles blown away. We were truly thankful.

The organizational process of the volunteer workers at the shelter amazed us. Upon entering the shelter, we received a smile and a cheerful “Hi, y’all.” We received a cot, pillow, blanket, and three hot meals per day for the two days we were in the shelter. The one meal that particularly stood out was on the first evening. We were served canned spaghetti with a slice of white bread smashed on top of the spaghetti.

For an Italian, this was very amusing. You get what you pay for, so we were grateful for the free dinner.

Several weeks later, my wife and I were visiting friends in a secluded area of North Carolina. We spotted a quaint local country store. I was amused at the sign over the front door of the store. "Bogs, Hogs, Logs, and Frogs." How unlike New York, I thought.

Afterward, I noticed a sign over a car repair shop that read, "Auto Repair Service. Free Pickup and Delivery. Try us once, and you'll never go anywhere again." Not exactly a confidence builder.

A few years earlier during our travels, we drove past a city park in Upstate New York during the winter. A sign read, "Closed for the season, reason, freezin'."

I am amused at what I see and hear every time I travel away from New York. It's truly wonderful to see so many talented individuals everywhere I go. I am also quick to notice the "crazies" who react in unusual ways to ordinary or mundane circumstances.

Life is a learning experience full of rich adventures. All we have to do is be willing to step out and look for them.

Before I became a world traveler, I served in the United States Army.

"For me, a painting is like a story which stimulates the imagination and draws the mind into a place filled with expectation, excitement, wonder and pleasure."

- J.P. Hughston

PART III

Uncle Sam Needs You!

Who Me?

16

You're in the Army Now

My entrance into the U.S. Army happened fortuitously with the first hint of autumn in the air. The year was 1958. In one week, my brother Nick got married, my brother Richie left for college, and I went into the Army. Suddenly my parents had to speak with each other again. My dad said the silence was deafening.

I had no idea what was ahead for me. Would I travel the world? Be stationed in some remote or exotic locale? Meet the president? Win a medal of honor? Learn a new skill? After all, I was a musician. I can't remember a time when music wasn't my life.

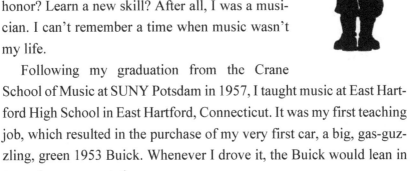

Following my graduation from the Crane School of Music at SUNY Potsdam in 1957, I taught music at East Hartford High School in East Hartford, Connecticut. It was my first teaching job, which resulted in the purchase of my very first car, a big, gas-guzzling, green 1953 Buick. Whenever I drove it, the Buick would lean in toward every gas station.

I rented a small apartment and began taking clarinet lessons with the principal clarinetist of the Hartford Symphony at the Hartt School of Music.

In 1957, news arrived that all able-bodied men would have to serve in the U.S. Army. If drafted, this meant serving for three years; if I enlisted for the draft, it meant two years. I opted for the two-year plan and entered in September following my first year of teaching. This way, I could be released from the Army in time to teach music beginning in the fall. It takes careful planning to place myself in a position where my music reigns supreme with a minimum of discomfort. After all, somebody had to defend our country....so why not me?

A Shot in the Arm

The Army (without my permission) assigned me to take basic training at Fort Dix, New Jersey. A busload of raw recruits arrived from Whitehall Street in New York City at a waiting station at Fort Dix, where they gave us a series of medical checkups and proceeded to give us shots for tetanus and other horrible diseases. Two Army medics approached us, one on each side, and injected us using a needle gun at the same time into both arms. I was shocked to see many of the big, strapping guys with huge, bulging muscles and tattoos faint when given the shots. I found it best not to look at the needles, but to think about something pleasant, like eating veal parmigiana and ziti or playing sax with a great jazz quartet. At any rate, this was the beginning of a long association with the United States Army.

After two days of physical and mental testing, I was assigned to a U.S. Army Infantry unit at Fort Dix, New Jersey. Most guys had their MOS (Main Operating Specialty), such as gunnery, heavy artillery, tanks, mortars, and the like. My MOS was saxophone!

The first day of Basic Training was a cool, breezy day in September 1958. The brown barracks looked like 200 outhouses strung together.

The stones in front of the barracks were painted bright white and read: "College of Knowledge."

About forty recruits were lined up in front of a stern-looking drill Sergeant Brill, who looked like he ate steel wool for breakfast. We called him "Brillo" behind his back. Sergeant Brill bellowed our names, as he read from a clipboard. "Bonavita, Carlone, Salvatori, Purcigliotti, Corozine, Cimino." We all replied, "Here," in a strident response.

He abruptly stopped. "What is this?" His countenance froze, and he screamed, "I've inherited a bunch of greasers and wops from the Mafia?"

He was so distressed that he began to kick rocks and stomp on the grass with his boots. It was like he had just been stung by 100 bees.

"I'm from the South," he roared. "Is there anybody here from the good ol' South?"

"I'm from the South," responded Tony Meads.

The sergeant gave Meads a life-size smile and aggressively and enthusiastically shook his hand, patting him on the back as he said, "Atta boy, Meads. I knew I liked you the moment I saw you. Tell me, Meads, what fine Southern city are you from? Let me guess...Memphis? New Orleans, How about Charleston? Are you a Charleston boy?"

"I'm from the South Bronx, sir!" Meads blurted out.

There was a long moment of silence, and then the volcano erupted. Sergeant Brill seethed and exploded in a rage quite unlike anything we had ever seen.

The sergeant began to scream at Meads and became so infuriated that his spittle sprayed all over Meads' face.

We naturally hooted at Meads' remark, so the sergeant had us run around the quarter-mile track four times with our hands above our heads yelling, "I love the South." Meads was given latrine duty every day for one week. The sergeant told Meads that the latrine was located in the "south" part of the barracks.

Being an adult and having somebody inspect me every day to make sure I put my clothes on properly and put my shoes on the right feet was a bit much.

Basic training lasted a grueling eight weeks. We learned to shoot a rifle, take 15-mile hikes, use a gas mask, throw hand grenades, and other such defensive and self-protective tactics of war. I took the rifle shooting and the proper use of the gas mask quite seriously. I figured these two items could save my life someday. The other stuff I didn't pay much attention to.

PREPARE FOR THE UNEXPECTED

One unforgettable incident happened near the beginning of basic training. All 300 recruits were sitting on freshly painted green wooden bleachers during a training session. A hard-nosed, meticulously attired paratrooper lieutenant led the session. He told us he was going to instruct us on how to use hand grenades.

As he began his presentation, he remarked, "Hand grenades are not toys." Regardless of what you see and hear in war movies, the hand-grenade pin cannot be pulled out using your teeth. "It takes all the muscle in your strongest arm to pull it. Don't believe that John Wayne movie stuff."

He then pulled the pin from the grenade. We looked around attentively.

"As long as I hold the lever close to the grenade," he continued, "it won't explode. You could walk around all day holding a grenade with the pin removed."

We continued to watch this "spit-and-polished" army officer walk around with a live grenade in his hand with the pin removed!

"But once you release the lever…" To our horror, he tossed the grenade under the stands where we were sitting. Suddenly 300 guys leaped, bounded, jumped, and dove off the bleachers. Luckily, no one was injured.

The hand grenade was a dud and didn't explode, which the lieutenant thought was amusing. "In war, you have to be prepared for the unexpected," which was how he ended the session.

This lieutenant is high on my list of clockwise walkers known as "Crazies."

17

FORWARD MARCH!

It is a fact that troops can march more effectively and get less weary if they keep in step to a steady beat. That is, except when crossing a bridge. The regular vibrations of 300 men crossing a bridge in step could cause the bridge to collapse. We marched "broken step" whenever we crossed a bridge.

When the sergeants found out I was an experienced music teacher and marching band director (I had one year of teaching under my belt), they asked me to organize a marching band from among the company's 300 recruits. I asked for volunteers and recruited 18 guys who were more than eager to play. A few were professional musicians who had played with some of the top big bands, while others were amateur musicians who played in high school or college. I quickly put together some marches, and we began rehearsing.

Colonel Haverstraw, the unit commander, was a southern gentleman from Atlanta and had approved the formation of the band.

"Corozine," he bellowed with a southern drawl, "I have one favor to ask."

"Anything, sir,"

"I have a favorite song I would like you to play every time you perform."

"Yes, sir. What song might that be, sir?"

"'Dixie'. I love that song. It stirs my blood to new heights of patriotism."

"Yes sir, 'Dixie' is also one of my favorite songs. It will be done as you wish, sir."

"Good. Feel free to schedule band rehearsals whenever you need them."

"Yes, sir. Thank you, sir."

"But remember, 'Dixie' has got to sound *special*."

"It will, sir. It will."

"Remember, teamwork is a lot of people doing what I say!"

This automatically put him into the category of a "Crazy." Now I suddenly had a lot more authority and influence than when I arrived. I could now, in some ways, control the fate of 18 musicians plus myself and stir the blood of my commander.

Considerable planning and coordination were required, much of it having nothing to do with actual music. We rehearsed a lot, particularly on cold, rainy days or when the company had to crawl on the ground carrying rifles. I believed, as did all the band members, that some of our most productive rehearsals took place on these cold, rainy days.

On a Wednesday, I called a special rehearsal because the company had a detail (extra assignment). They were told to "police the area," which meant that everybody (except the band) had to walk around the base for two hours picking up cigarette butts and other debris. We had a great two-hour rehearsal that day.

On another occasion, the entire company was scheduled to take a 15-mile hike with instruments, rifles, backpacks, helmets, and other paraphernalia. The band played six marches (on a rotating basis) including "Dixie", for the entire 15 miles. To accomplish this daunting task, 18 soldiers were selected and ordered to carry the rifles and backpacks belonging to the band members. We carried and played only our musical instruments. Our great musical expertise did not compensate for the angst we caused those 18 soldiers.

I couldn't call band rehearsals all day, every day. We were also required to attend classes, be prepared for barracks inspections, show up for routine infantry exercises, pass our physical training, and attend other related duties. After all, we were in the Army.

At one point, it got to where the musicians were asking and prompting me to call extra rehearsals for almost any reason. I quickly realized they were asking for reasons not directly related to the quality or excellence of the band.

"It's going to be 85 degrees today… isn't this a good day to rehearse?" was not an unusual request.

I listened attentively to each heartfelt request, and most of the time, I did call a special rehearsal. After all, I wanted to keep the morale of band members at a high level. My college psychology professor always said that a happy and contented person responds better than a miserable one. I always try to use whatever I learn to support the situation at hand.

MARCH TO NOWHERE

My buddy, Jerry Puleo, was a professional trumpet player from New York City and performed with many famous big jazz bands. He played the lead trumpet in our band, and commanded the respect of the other band musicians.

One early morning in October, while we were preparing ourselves and our music for a 15-mile hike, Jerry came to me with an out-of-the-ordinary request. He said, "Schwartz." He called me that because I reminded him of a shrewd lawyer he knew in New York. "I can't stand not being able to practice. Playing those six marches for every parade for the 15-mile marches is getting to me, especially 'Dixie.' If I hear that song again, I'm going to jump off the nearest bridge. Besides, I don't have any serious time to practice anymore."

I listened attentively, realizing that the nearest bridge was only four feet above a slow-moving stream. Nevertheless, I appreciated what he was going through.

"Schwartz, how about if I start the parade with the band, and as we turn the first corner near the end of the barracks, I slip into the barracks and practice my trumpet all day till you guys return."

Realizing I was responsible for the sound quality of the band and the attendance of the players at all functions. I said, "Jerry, go for it! We can play the music with the other four trumpet players playing the melody. If the melody is strong, no one will notice one player is missing."

Jerry did just that. We rounded the first corner of the barracks, Jerry silently slipped into the empty barracks and practiced trumpet for the rest of the day while we marched and sweated.

Upon our return to the base, we approached the barracks where Jerry was practicing. Without a sound and some smudged dirt on his pants, he got in line with the band and played along with us for the final 100 yards of our march.

At the end of the march, he commented to the sergeant how tiring the march was. The sergeant gave him a concerned look but was none the wiser. Thankfully, Jerry had gotten to practice and was satisfied. We played for the 15-mile march and were satisfied. The sergeants appeared to be as well. The only unhappy souls were the soldiers who had to carry our rifles and backpacks.

A term for what Jerry did is called "Goldbricking" (inventing excuses to shirk one's duties). However, the morale of the band was elevated because Jerry sounded better than ever, and the band had a good laugh listening to Jerry recap the story.

MEET MY FRIEND!

While struggling through basic training at Fort Dix, New Jersey, plagued with terrible food, besieged with 15-mile marches, running up and down hills with a rifle and backpack, and listening to the constant use of curse words by the troops, I longed for my mother's pasta and encouraging words. Tom Anthony, a college buddy from SUNY Potsdam, contacted me and asked me to come over to his barracks on Sunday to meet his new friend.

Puzzled by his request, but also glad to hear from him, I went to Barracks #29 on Sunday at 3 p.m. expecting to meet Godzilla or someone incredibly strange. Tom was a musical guy, who played piano, and trumpet, sang, and made friends quite easily, but his quirky sense of humor often got him in hot water.

For instance, at Potsdam, there was a tall beacon-light tower that spread a glitter of light over most of the campus. Tom and his three fraternity buddies decided to replace the yellow-tinted light at the top of the tower with a red blinking light. They cautiously approached the tower at midnight, hoisted a huge ladder and ropes with pulleys, and Tom ascended to the top. The students thought it was a cool move while the faculty and administration grimaced in pain. This was the topic of discussion and laughter for the remainder of the semester. Administration never found out who perpetrated this prank.

Upon arriving, Tom introduced me to Steve Lawrence, the popular jazz vocalist who was assigned to Tom's barracks. Steve was a very hip and comical guy from Brooklyn, New York, and we talked for some time. He told me that after basic training was over, he would be doing concerts for the troops for the Special Services section of the Army.

At that moment, a pretty young girl showed up and ran to Steve, giving him a big kiss. It was his wife, Eydie Gormé, also a great singer. She was visiting him, which was allowed on weekends. They both sang as a duo on Steve Allen's *Tonight Show* in the 1950s and had been recently married.

Eydie was gracious and easy to talk to. Her positive outlook on life was refreshing after listening to the complaints of the enlisted men in my company. It was a glorious afternoon for me. I hated to leave such hip folks to go back to my barracks smothered in gloom and despair.

Tom Anthony went on to be one of the most successful producers and composers of jingles in New York. He later retired and now owns a horse farm in Wyoming.

18

Body Odor Can Do You In!

The Army was gung-ho about how we appeared physically but casual about how we smelled beneath our uniforms.

Our frequent inspections were about neatness. Our uniforms were clean and pressed, our metal belt buckles were shiny and glowing, and our dress shoes were spit-polished to a glowing shade of black.

Spud Jenks was a recruit who hailed from the hills of Arkansas, where hygiene was not a topic of conversation. His real name was Spaulding, but he preferred to be called Spud. He hadn't worn such fine clothes in a long time, perhaps never. Spud refused to take a shower, so after a few weeks, we assisted him. After three weeks of no showers, we could no longer stand the smell emanating from his body, so six of us grabbed him, stripped him, carried him into the shower (while holding our breath), and scrubbed him with a wooden handle brush. Spud quickly got the idea. From that moment on, he never failed to take a shower.

In some obscure way, we believe we helped Spud understand the importance of personal hygiene.

A Close Shave

Freddy Bovino was another popular recruit. He wasn't the brightest guy in the world, but he had a warm personality. He came from Forest Hills, Queens, New York, and had great difficulty adjusting to Army traditions and protocol.

All recruits were required to shave daily and inspected by our platoon sergeant. Freddy habitually overslept and seldom had time to shave properly for morning inspection. He often failed the shaving portion of the inspection and was ordered to run around the track with a straight razor in his right hand and shave (with no shaving cream) until his face was clean-shaven. Each time, he returned with blood all over his face. We helped clean him before classes. One of us volunteered to help Freddy pass the exams and correctly follow instructions so he could pass basic training. If he failed basic training, he had to repeat the entire eight weeks.

Freddy had narrow escapes with the rifle on the rifle range. He often pointed his rifle in the wrong direction, with everybody yelling to hit the dirt. Once, he dropped a live grenade due to nerves. The sergeant quickly picked it up and threw it for him. He inhaled instead of exhaled while using the gas mask and the sergeants had to drag him by his feet into fresh air to revive him. Freddy could never quite understand how things were supposed to be done in the Army.

Happily, Freddy made it through basic training and graduated with us. He was so proud of his accomplishment, and we were for him.

Army Comic

The axiom "Laughter is the best medicine" came from Proverbs 17:22—*A merry heart does good, like medicine.*

Laughter is aerobic, meaning it increases the oxygen intake in your body and helps reduce stress levels by relaxing your muscles. It also has been known to lower blood pressure, boost the immune system, and produce a surge of energy running through the entire body. One physician described laughter as "inner jogging" and believes that laughter is good for our cardiovascular system.

Our platoon sergeant had a sign above his barracks door. "There's no problem that can't be solved by the use of high explosives." We certainly got the hint and left him alone as much as possible. I venture to say that he walked clockwise.

Medical research has suggested that happy individuals recover from diseases much more quickly than complaining patients. I believe people who laugh a lot live longer and more fulfilling lives.

One particular guy, Junior Smalls, always seemed to get into trouble. During a barracks inspection, he was found with a "Holiday Inn" towel in his footlocker. For that, we all had to do 50 push-ups and police the barracks area for cigarette butts.

Junior Smalls loved to play tricks and practical jokes. Some mornings, at about 2 or 3 a.m., he would crawl on his hands and knees from the barracks, about 200 yards, to the loudspeaker system located in the center of the inspection area. He proceeded to turn on the amplifier, plug in the microphone, and squawk like a chicken over the loudspeaker waking everybody in the unit. He would then run back to his bunk and pretend he was fast asleep.

The lights went on in all the barracks. The sergeants got us up, in our underwear, in a straight line. They asked repeatedly who did this thing. Nobody responded, but we all laughed under our breath. During the next few weeks, the platoon sergeants tried to catch the culprit in action. Junior Smalls always outsmarted them. He would select opportune times to pull his pranks. Since we covered for him every time, Junior Smalls never was caught.

A Real Blast

Junior Smalls also made us believe that live hand grenades were blowing up. If a sergeant walked by, Junior Smalls would gently pull the invisible grenade pin and roll the imaginary grenade toward the sergeant. Smalls would jump into the air when it was supposed to explode. Of course, this got everybody laughing, and often, we got extra push-ups.

One day he pulled this stunt at a big formal review of the troops by the colonels. When the colonels arrived (we called them the "scrambled eggs" due to the yellow markings on their hats), Junior Smalls would toss a few imaginary grenades under their feet, put his fingers in his ears, wait five seconds, and then jump in the air as if an explosion had taken place. We naturally found this amusing and began to laugh, smile, or smirk at the antics. The colonels considered our conduct inappropriate, and the entire company had to police (clean) the area for two days.

19

No Class

We were required to attend classes during the day with titles such as "How to Take Apart and Reassemble Your Rifle," "How to Properly Use a Gas Mask," and other topics dealing with safety and survival.

I could never quite understand Army logic. We were told never to interrupt or to ask questions of the instructor who presented the lectures. The lectures were lengthy and mind-numbing. The facts, in most cases, were irrelevant to real life.

After having spent four years in college and one-year teaching music in high school, I had a pretty good idea of what constituted good and bad teaching. This was an example of bad teaching. Questions were not allowed, and few practical illustrations were presented.

However, during one lecture, my buddy Richard Epstein raised his hand and asked a question right in the middle of the lecture. The instructor was perplexed and stopped teaching. A few moments passed, and then the instructor started at the beginning of the lecture! We were aghast…a memorized presentation with no understanding…mindless rote teaching…yuk!

I must admit that our sergeant was on target once that I could remember. One day he asked us, “Two soldiers were bunking down in the field for the night. If you were one of the soldiers and I asked you, ‘when you see all the stars in the sky, what do you think?’”

Ira Shulman blurted out. “Well, I think of how insignificant we are in the universe; how small a piece of such a grand design. I can’t help but wonder if what we do truly means anything or makes any difference. Why? What do you think of, Sarge?”

“I would think somebody stole the damn tent.”

We all had a good laugh at that.

One time the sergeant said, “Dress uniforms will be strictly optional, and that’s an order.”

We were told three things throughout our days in the Army: One, there is the right way, there is a wrong way, and there is the Army way. This was the Army way.

My former sergeant and more than a few Army vets probably walk clockwise around the mall.

HAPPY BIRTHDAY!

Not everything in the Army was fun and games. On my 23rd birthday, I was in basic training away from home. I didn’t tell anyone it was my birthday. Suddenly one of the sergeants came into the barracks and announced that our barracks would have a GI party after dinner, beginning around 7 p.m.

I thought, “Cool idea.” Maybe they’ll have a cake, with candles and balloons. Maybe someone found out it was my birthday; after all, I’m the leader of the company band…”

I abruptly found out that a GI party meant we had to clean the barracks, wash the walls, and scrub the floors and windows. The aim was to prepare the old wooden barracks for the following day’s inspection. Inspection is where the company commander arrives with his assistants with clipboards, all wearing white gloves, looking for hidden dirt or dust. They would try to bounce a quarter off the bunk blankets and inspect our uniforms. If we didn't pass an inspection, we could be given "details" such as "policing" the area, another GI party, or raking leaves for two days. Most days we did okay with the resulting punishment motivating us to give our best effort.

BEARER OF BAD NEWS (BBN)

Colin MacDonald was a professional clarinetist, but he was a BBN (Bearer of Bad News). Every time he was around, we would hear about the latest tragedies in the news, or worse yet, about the unpleasant things we could look forward to doing.

Things like: "Hey guys, did you know we have a 15-mile hike on Wednesday beginning at 6 a.m.?" or "Leave has been canceled due to a visiting general coming on base and we will be marching in a parade tomorrow," or "They scheduled a GI party tomorrow night to get us ready for inspection the next day."

Whenever Colin was around, the other guys tried to avoid him, not listen, or just shout some expletives in his direction. He was like the dark cloud of death hanging over us.

I don't know why anybody would be a BBN, but Colin sure seemed to enjoy the reaction he got when he blurted out a rotten detail or terrible event coming.

One breezy morning in October, Colin and I were sitting outside the barracks cleaning our rifles.

"Vince, guess what will happen if we don't assemble our rifle in the prescribed amount of time?" remarked Colin.

"I don't care," I replied, "I'm going to do it within the amount of time prescribed."

"But what if you don't?"

"Don't worry. I will!"

I don't know where Colin MacDonald works today, but my guess is he works for the Internal Revenue Service!

Drug-Free Zone

Often friends will ask me, "Being a musician, how did you manage to stay away from taking drugs?"

I never felt I needed to take "downers," "uppers," or "pot" to enhance my life.

One day while rehearsing with a six-piece jazz combo at Fort Dix, I was offered a marijuana cigarette to smoke by Glenn Dow, the bass player.

I asked, "What good will it do me?"

He answered, "Man, it's the craziest, daddio. It lifts you to the heavens and sends you over the moon."

I replied, "My personality is up enough, and I sure don't need any help to feel better about life." I have always been an optimistic person. So, I politely refused his offer by stating, "Not for me!"

He roared, "Man, you're losing out on a thing man, a real thing, and you'll play your horn better too."

Well, I never did find out what that "thing" was, and I noticed others did not play better when on drugs; they just *thought* they played better.

20

THERE'S GOTTA BE A WAY!

HOME, SWEET HOME

Most weekends, I booked playing gigs with my jazz band back in my hometown of Peekskill, New York. I had to figure out how to get a leave every weekend. To backtrack, during my school years, my brother Nick and I used to compete in push-up contests every night before bedtime. We got to the point where we could both do 150 push-ups in a row. My brother was much better at doing push-ups. Nick could do push-ups using only one hand and by quickly clapping both hands together between push-ups. I attempted this feat, and I landed on my nose. I never attempted any of these maneuvers again. We did push-ups every night for about five years during our junior high and high school years. I didn't realize then how valuable this skill would become in the future.

To earn a pass home for a weekend, our company held push-up contests. Whoever did the most push-ups got to go home for the weekend. I saw an opportunity to win the battle against a seemingly hopeless and discouraging situation.

The first weekend some guy did 48 push-ups, and I did 49. I went home for the weekend to play jazz. I earned a pass every weekend. The highest number of push-ups I had to do was 88. I beat out a huge guy as the troops yelped and shouted. I even remember a few of the guys betting on who would win. Whenever I saw the other guy cave in and give up, I did exactly one more push-up to beat him. I never told anybody how many I could do.

Most weekend passes began at noon Friday, and we were to report to the base by Monday morning before 8 a.m.

Fridays were an open night for me because most jazz gigs occurred Saturdays. So, I usually had a date on Friday evening.

Susan Fitzpatrick was a girl of extraordinary beauty and intelligence—elegant, svelte, charming, and a little erudite. She came from a family of doctors and dentists, and had discriminating tastes in clothes, food, cars, and friends.

I guess she went out with me because I was, as she put it, "Exciting, a jazz saxophone player, a bit crazy, and not boring."

Friday, I decided to take Susan to an elegant French restaurant, La Fontaine, nestled in the woods of lower Westchester County near Scarsdale, a wealthy suburb of New York City.

Earlier that day, I washed and waxed my 1953 green Buick. I even washed off the seats, sprayed peppermint air freshener inside the car, and borrowed my dad's Old Spice aftershave. I was raring to go!

Upon entering the restaurant, I handed the maître d de a five-dollar bill, and he immediately showed us to a nice table overlooking green pastures.

We were next served appetizers we didn't ask for, while we perused the fancy menu. Alas, the menu was in French, and I could only interpret Italian terms.

Not wanting to appear ignorant or unsophisticated in front of Susan, I scanned the menu, pointing with my finger as I read, and commented aloud with statements like, "This is good if not overcooked" and "This has to be very fresh." Susan was impressed with my apparent knowledge of the French language.

"Where did you learn to speak French?" she asked.

"Oh, I picked it up by listening to my friends and watching French movies."

A tuxedoed waiter approached our table and asked in French what we would like to order. At least, I assumed that's what he said.

I smiled and pointed to the menu, "We'll take two of those."

The waiter responded tersely in English, "I'm sorry, sir, that is the manager."

Was I embarrassed? Somewhat, but I told Susan that my friends had never used the word "manager" in my presence, which was why I didn't recognize it.

I don't know if she believed me, but she seemed amused by the entire incident.

We ordered filet mignon, rare. Upon seeing my portion, I said to the waiter, "Pardon, my filet mignon seems to be very small."

With an irritated smirk, he replied, "It's not small, sir. We recently expanded the size of the dining room."

He thought this was a funny remark. Susan and I got a kick out of his response.

Was the food expensive? I found an oyster in my oyster soup, and I almost broke even!

What happened to Susan Fitzpatrick? She married a government lawyer, and the last time I heard, they were living outside of Washington, D.C.

MORSE CODE: I'M AN EXPERT!

Being a musician helped me in other ways. One dreary, rainy-day Sergeant Brill asked if anybody wanted to take a test to be a Morse code operator. My knowledge of Morse code was limited, except I knew that

Samuel Morse invented it in 1844. I also remembered that Morse was a portrait painter.

Not caring particularly about being a Morse code operator, I along with 10 or 12 of my friends, volunteered to take the exam. We were promptly escorted to another building. I found that taking written exams often exempted us from doing other scheduled mundane duties.

The exam consisted of tapping back a sequence of dots and dashes (aural blips). Each exercise got progressively longer and presumably more difficult. I didn't have much difficulty with any of it as I tapped what I heard.

I thought, "Once you understand Morse code, a tap dancer will drive you crazy."

After the exam was over, Sergeant Mulroney summoned me to his office. "Corozine, who taught you Morse code?"

"Nobody, sir."

"Well, where did you learn Morse Code?"

"I didn't, sir. This was my first exposure to it."

"I don't understand…"

"Understand what, sir?"

"You're the first person to get 100 percent on the Morse Code exam."

"It was easy, sir."

"Why?"

"I'm a musician. The beeps and blips played are basic rhythms to me. I simply tapped back what I heard."

"I think you would make a good Morse code operator, Corozine."

"I don't think so, sir."

"Why not?"

I deemed it my duty to explain, which I did, "My MOS is saxophone, sir. I'd rather play the rhythms on my saxophone than tap them on a machine."

"Return to your unit. You're excused, soldier," he said abruptly.

I returned to my barracks, chuckling as I went.

21

Army Gourmet

During basic training, all recruits were occasionally expected to "pull" KP (kitchen police) duty. If you saw your name on the KP roster for the next day, you were required to tie a white towel at the end of your bedpost before going to bed.

I remember the wind began to stir around midnight. I could hear the rain pelting against the barracks window. At precisely 4:30 am, the sergeant roused us out of our sleep. As the wind stiffened and heavy rains flooded the streets, we were promptly escorted to the mess hall that contained a large steel vegetable cooler. We were expected to remove all the crates of vegetables from the frigid cooler. Next, we had to wash the walls and floors of the cooler and return the crates of vegetables to their rightful place as we shivered in the cold air. This lasted until 6 a.m.

At 6 a.m., we washed our hands with strong brown soap and began loading slices of white bread into the enormous toasters in preparation for breakfast. The toasters worked on a conveyor belt where slices of bread rotated around and around. Some of the guys cooked eggs and bacon as directed by a gruff Army cook.

A delicacy was SOS (creamy chipped beef smothered in a white sauce served on toast) along with other delightful morsels. I could never get myself to try it.

I did, however, notice a clever sign posted in the mess hall in a non-smoking area. It read, “If we see you smoke, we will assume you are on fire and take appropriate action.”

The company entered for breakfast between 6:30 and 7 a.m. After breakfast, we cleaned the tables, placed the dishes in the huge dishwashers, scrubbed the floors, washed the windows, hosed down the walls, and cleaned anything else in view. We even enjoyed the company of a crusty Army cook, who gave us precise orders on how to “police” (clean) the area.

At about 9 a.m., we were permitted a 15-minute break. Most guys went outside to smoke, or in my case, I laid down on top of sacks of potatoes and took a short snooze. I noticed one guy leaning against a wall, sighing, blowing smoke, and wincing from the pain of working in the kitchen. After our break, we began to peel potatoes, skin carrots, shell beans, and do anything our charming cook told us.

The morning passed slowly. Lunch began at 11:30 a.m. and continued until 1 p.m. After lunch, we went through the same routine scrubbing the floors, washing the windows, and hosing down the walls. Everything still looked clean from the previous scrubbing. My love for working in the kitchen was short-lived.

After dinner, we cleaned up, and again washed the floors, windows, and walls. Everything looked sterile and antiseptic. We were excused around 7:30 p.m., exhausted and relieved. To this day, I admire cooks, but I never want to be one.

Religion Helps!

One dreary, rain-soaked Sunday in early November, I pulled KP duty again. There I was, the Catholic Italian with my four Jewish buddies, Richard Epstein, Ira Shulman, Sidney Levitz, and Dave Kappelwitz.

At about 9 a.m., Sergeant Kent asked who would be going to Sunday Mass at the Catholic chapel. Of course, I being Catholic, wanted to go. Suddenly, my four Jewish buddies raised their hands. They wanted to go to the Catholic Mass too. They saw the advantage of being a Catholic for two hours.

"Are you guys Catholic?" asked a puzzled-looking Sergeant Kent.

"Yeah, Sarge," replied wise-mouthed Epstein, "we recently converted."

"Yeah, that's what we did," added Shulman, "we're now good Catholics."

"Yeah," responded Kappelwitz, "my father married an ex-nun."

Before he could put his foot further into his mouth, exposing himself as a fraud, and nix the deal, I said, "That's right, Sarge, I can vouch for them. They're all Catholic."

"Okay, let's go," muttered Sergeant Kent.

As he led us out the door, we happily exited from the mess hall to the Army vehicle en route to the Catholic chapel.

We called Sergeant Kent "Clark" behind his back. We made comments like, "He'll jump into his Superman outfit as soon as he can find a phone booth he can fit into."

Sergeant Kent was a bit paunchy around the waist and flabby around the buttocks and loved to eat raspberry-filled donuts.

Another time, when he was being particularly obnoxious and nasty to us, Epstein suggested that he practice flying off the tallest building on the base. Sergeant Kent was not amused by this comment. Epstein had to shine everybody's dress shoes in the barracks for two days. A mouth shut does have its advantages.

En route to the church, my Jewish friends asked me what they should know and what they should do during the service.

I told them, "Watch me closely and do everything I do. I told them, "Don't even think about it; just do what I do."

In the church, I sat in the middle, flanked by Epstein and Kappelwitz on my left with Shulman and Levitz on my right. To our dismay,

Sergeant Kent was sitting directly behind us and could easily watch our every move.

My buddies watched me intently and imitated everything I did. I dipped my finger in holy water when entering the church, genuflected, made the sign of the cross, picked up a hymnal, put 25 cents into the offering plate, stood up, sat down, repeated phrases in Latin after the priest, and performed other motions that Catholics are accustomed to doing at mass.

Suddenly, I put my hand to my mouth and coughed three times. You guessed it. All four of my Jewish friends put their hands to their mouths and coughed three times. I found this particularly amusing and now chuckle whenever I think of it. Sergeant Kent didn't catch this one.

On another day, Sergeant Kent assigned me to garbage detail. He told me that my comments that day about the Army were not funny. This meant I had to empty the garbage into the properly indicated garbage bin and make sure that no other person deposited garbage into the wrong bin. I was guarding the garbage bins while holding my nose with the thumb and first finger of my right hand. The containers were labeled "Edible" and "Non-edible." A paradox in terms. I concluded, "Waste is a terrible thing to mind."

Friends In High Places

After experiencing my first KP duty, I quickly concluded these were good days to schedule band rehearsals. However, one Wednesday when I couldn't wrangle a rehearsal, my name was put on the KP duty roster. Immediately I got on the phone and called my boyhood friend, Mike Nardone, who was two years older than me. Mike was stationed at Fort Dix. He had a higher rank than I did. I thought he could help me out of this predicament. He asked me the time and location of my KP duty.

When the day came, I arrived at the mess hall kitchen around 5 a.m., already exhausted and dragging my tail. We immediately entered the frigid vegetable cooler and emptied it. Next, we washed the walls and floor of the cooler and then replaced the wooden boxes of vegetables. It was nearly 6 a.m. Around breakfast time, my buddy Mike suddenly burst into the kitchen with four armed military police carrying rifles. Everybody saluted him due to his rank and shrank seeing the four-armed MPs. The cooks and my buddies looked worried and nervous.

Without cracking a smile, Mike yelled, "Corozine, where's Corozine?" in a booming, demanding, authoritative bass voice.

"Here, sir." I timidly raised my hand, cowering with a meek, whimpering reply.

Mike had great difficulty not smiling and smirking at my nervous, quivering response. "Come with me now!"

"Yes, sir," I said as I feigned a frightened look.

The four MPs surrounded me with rifles leveled at me and began to count aloud as we marched out of the kitchen. I could tell Mike was quite amused by this charade. He deserved an Oscar.

No doubt, the cooks and other soldiers in the kitchen thought I did something terrible, and I was being escorted to the brig. For the rest of the day, Mike and I played cards, drank soda, and had a great laugh. When asked by my friends what happened, I replied, "It was a case of mistaken identity." Perhaps for the first time, I was proud to have outsmarted the Army.

22

Danger

Before graduating from basic training, all recruits had to complete the dreaded Infiltration Course. This meant we had to crawl on our stomachs with our rifles across our arms while wearing a backpack and metal helmet for 100 yards. This occurred on a frigid November night. The noise, confusion, and bedlam surrounded me as I crawled to make it to the end of the course.

To get a pass for the weekend, we had to complete the course without getting any dirt on our rifle barrels. Realizing this was difficult to achieve, I needed a strategy to escape Fort Dix and be home that weekend. I promptly phoned Mike Nardone and asked him for advice. He said, "Put a piece of cotton in the rifle barrel before you begin the course and take it out quickly before the Sergeant inspects your rifle at the end of the course."

With deafening explosions going off in bunkers, we crawled. Brilliant flares lit up the sky. We froze in position. Actual bullets shot over our heads. We were tense and nervous. This real-war simulation experience was all too real. They advised us never to stand up while maneuvering through the course.

"The bullets will be coming from machine guns," we were told, "shooting real bullets about five feet above your head. If you stand up, the bullets will go through you, and you will have no more weekend passes." I found out later the bullets were aimed 8-10 feet above our heads.

Thank God nobody stood up or panicked under these war-like conditions. I made it twisting my body under the barbed wire, sliding forward in the dirt on my back while pushing the barbed wire above my head with my rifle.

Promptly, I removed the wad of cotton from my rifle barrel. I proudly extended my rifle to the sergeant. He inspected my rifle a couple times, wrote my name, and said, "Corozine, you did it again. You earn a pass to go home." Success! I love the sweet smell of cotton in the mornings.

Promotion

Following basic training, I opted for and was selected to go to advanced music school at Fort Dix. Mike arranged this for me. He asked where I wanted to go after basic, and I told him to any music school not too far away from New York. A few days later, he told me it was all set. His buddy, Frank Napoli took care of all the details.

As it turned out, I was the only one in the company of 300 men selected to go to advanced music school at Fort Dix. After calling out 299 men by name and destination, I was the only one remaining. I was standing all alone as the sergeant looked at me, puzzled, and asked, "Corozine, how the hell did you pull this off?"

"Dunno, Sarge. I guess I'm just lucky," I replied, shrugging my shoulders.

Upon reporting to the advanced music school, I found the content of the courses to be on par with my first year at college. I took all the placement exams and whizzed through them. I scored high as I did with my Morse code exam. Only this time, I understood and enjoyed what I was doing.

The officer in charge reviewed my qualifications and asked me to take charge of the jazz band. The Army produced a weekly radio show. They needed someone to write the musical arrangements and lead the band. In their opinion, I adequately filled both roles.

The officer in charge asked, "Corozine, do you think you can handle the job as described?"

"Easily, sir."

"Good for you."

"I'll take the job, sir."

"How about if I release you from all duties," he replied, "except to rehearse the band on Thursdays and Fridays. That way you can prepare for the radio show taped on Fridays."

"That'll work fine, sir," I said, "but where do I get the time to write the musical arrangements and copy the parts for the radio show each week?"

"Oh, I see. I can assign you to your private room with a piano and supply you with whatever you need to get the job done."

"That sounds reasonable to me, sir."

"Just let the supply sergeant know what you need to get the job done. In addition, remember we need four or five musical arrangements done each week."

I immediately went to the supply sergeant and requested score paper, copy paper, black ink, scotch tape, erasers, pencils, and other music writing supplies. The supply sergeant was annoyed that he had to go off base to requisition these special supplies since I needed them in a hurry.

I spent three days from 8 a.m. to 5 p.m. in the piano studio writing and copying music arrangements for the band. Thursday and Friday, I would rehearse the band for the Friday taping. I felt like the composer, Franz Josef Haydn, who, in 1761, took over as court composer at Esterhazy Palace as Assistant Kapellmeister of the orchestra in Eisenstadt.

He, too, was paid to write music and had a wonderful group of musicians to write for. I was in my glory!

The other sergeants were envious and resentful. I had a private room with an upright piano, and no duties during the week except to write music. No one was allowed to disturb me without the permission of the Commanding Officer. I was popular with the enlisted musicians but not with the regular Army personnel.

Most of our radio shows were taped for future broadcasting over Army radio. However, occasionally, on special holidays like Veteran's Day, we were asked to do a live show. This presented special problems in that we couldn't go back and correct mistakes. If a tempo was too slow or too fast, we had to live with it.

Our vocalist Bunny Morton was assigned to the band without my knowledge. She was a WAC (Women's Army Corps) lieutenant, and we found out later that she was dating one of the officers. She was under the impression that she could sing. She sang out of tune and often entered the wrong spot in the music.

After rehearsing a vocal arrangement, Bunny sang the classic song, "Laura," She would turn to the band, and glare and say, "Tsk, what a band," shaking her head in a derogatory manner. To put it mildly, her attitude did not make her popular with the band members. My buddy Jerry Puleo threatened to use her for target practice! I told Jerry that a season in the brig is not worth it. He agreed and calmed down. She continually hurled negative barbs at the band. One day, I got a brilliant idea. Retribution was at hand.

Bunny's vocal range was up to a "D" in the treble staff. The band members knew this very well. I made sure that her arrangements fit her vocal range.

One day while doing a live radio performance, I quietly told the band to transpose (raise) one of Bunny's vocal arrangements up a minor third. This meant she would have to sing one and a half steps higher than she was able to. Her high "D" now became a high "F." Bunny began to sing and when she came to the high note, she couldn't reach it. She sounded like someone choking a chicken!

She was embarrassed. After the show, the band members said, shaking their heads, "Tsk, what a singer!

DID YOU ASK ME?

The service bands are perhaps the finest band in the U.S. We moved from Carmel, New York to the Annapolis, Maryland area in 2015. I was privileged to have these musicians playing in my Annapolis Jazztet, which consisted of trumpet, sax, trombone, piano, bass, and a drummer who also sings.

I quickly found out these players were at the same musicianship level as the West Point Band, in which I spent two years of my life and wrote music for them for ten years after leaving the Army.

Someone suggested I contact the leader of the Chesapeake Grays Big Band, comprising 18 retired musicians from the U.S. Military Academy Band. The band leader asked me to bring arrangements (charts) to their rehearsals and conduct the band.

The musicians in the West Point band could play notes following a fly walking up the page. The Navy musicians in Annapolis had the same level of musical proficiency.

While rehearsing the Chesapeake Grays Big Band, I stopped the band and asked if the tempo felt right or did they think it would be better if we played a little faster. I waited and no response, so I asked again. No response. I was puzzled by this but continued to the next song.

During the break, the bass trombone player came up to me and said, "Vince, you must remember that most of us have been in the Navy band for 25-35 years…and in all that time, no conductor has ever asked our opinion!"

I was surprised by his remark, but after I thought about my experience in the West Point Band, he was right! The Army has a chain of command or division of labor that is quite rigid. No one at a lower rank ever makes suggestions unless asked, and even then, it is quite rare. I guess their motto could be, "I conduct, you play and have no say!"

Some of the finest musical experiences I have ever had were when I was a member of the West Point Band.

23

New Vistas

My second eight weeks of advanced music training were ending, and I became concerned about where I would spend the remainder of my two years in the Army. For once, I was stumped. Up to this point, I depended on Mike and my ingenuity to keep me clear of potential problems or unpleasant situations. What I wanted most was to continue with my music, but I certainly didn't want to wind up in some cold geographic area in Minnesota or Alaska. Realizing that most Army musicians are assigned to basebands in remote areas of the United States where the quality of musicianship is mediocre, I needed a new approach and strategy. The means for achieving this aim were unclear, but I refused to give up hope.

Fortunately, one of the musicians informed me that the USMA Band at West Point was looking for musicians. They had the reputation of being the finest band in the U.S. Army, and West Point was only eight miles from my home across the Hudson River. What an opportunity.

Seven musicians from our band silently stole away early one afternoon, and without permission, we journeyed to West Point to audition for the band. We were all accepted.

My parents were pleased with my assignment to the West Point band because I could now live at home and play jazz on weekends. No more push-up contests!

The West Point Band performed for Army football games, cadet parades, concerts, and other musical functions at Eisenhower Hall and Trophy Point overlooking the magnificent Hudson River. I left West Point with respect for our flag, our traditions, and our rich American heritage.

However, my wacky sense of humor almost got me into trouble. I put in a formal request for "Overseas Pay" because I had to cross the Hudson River at the Bear Mountain Bridge each day to get to West Point. You guessed it; Colonel Smythe was not amused at my request.

One day I was summoned to his office following a band rehearsal.

He said, "Corozine, you should be proud to be in the band and shouldn't be concerned about non-musical matters." He felt I was pushing the envelope.

Despite his irritation with me, he told me I was a good bandsman, and I was to fill my time with musical duties and forget about other things.

"Yes, sir," I respectfully responded.

"You are excused," he said.

I saluted and left his office, pondering what had just transpired.

Nevertheless, the "Army way" prevailed. I was lucky. There were no further incidents during my brief Army career.

Unfortunately, not all folks have the same admiration for amusing and anecdotal stories that I have. In recalling this incident a few years later, I remembered James Thurber as he described humor as emotional chaos remembered in tranquility.

Later, as a civilian, I composed and arranged music for the West Point Jazz Knights, did guest conducting, and frequently traveled summers with them for ten years.

Push-ups, parades, practicing, policing, and people were what the Army was all about. Before I served in the United States Army, I got an education.

PART IV

SCHOOL DAZE

"The world of reality has its limits;
the world of imagination is boundless."

- Jean-Jacques Rousseau

24

I'M A LEARNER

"I got an A in philosophy because I proved that
my professor didn't exist."
- Judy Tenata

Redwood trees last for a thousand years. A face-lift lasts for six to ten years, a dollar bill one year, and a painted line on the road for four months. However, an education lasts a lifetime—at least the ability to learn does.

Unlike medicine, law, or nuclear physics, we all have attended school, and therefore, we often claim to know what changes or educational improvements are needed.

I am impelled to suggest that educators often perpetuate the same organizational system that brought them success. I find that our educational system is an anachronistic art that is slow to change due to the entrenchment of educators and their reluctance to revise the learning system.

"We think too much about effective methods of
teaching and not enough about effective methods of learning."
- John Carolus S.J.

Research shows that we forget the first 50% of what we hear immediately, 80% within twenty-four hours, and 97% within a week.

The memorization of facts may certainly win prizes on quiz programs and in trivia contests, but it has little value without being able to reason or apply them to life's situations. I am convinced some of the worst teaching is done at the university level, where the teacher lectures, seldom asking questions or encouraging feedback. Educators must provoke students and present opportunities to think for themselves, inquire about and ferret out multiple solutions to a problem, and reason from an intelligent base of knowledge.

"Spoon-feeding, in the long run,
teaches us nothing but the shape of the spoon."
- E.M. Forster

IN THE BEGINNING...

My experience in school was generally a positive one. I spent thirteen years in public schools, an additional four years in undergraduate school to obtain my bachelor's degree, and another eight years in graduate school (part-time) to earn my master's and professional diploma—all in music and music education.

NAMM (National Association of Music Merchants) has funded scientific research that links music-making and physical, social, and psychological well-being. Its research and research by other groups, concluded that making music can exercise the brain, increase productivity, fight memory loss, reduce stress, lower blood pressure, and stave off depression. *(Making Music Jan/Feb 2007 pg.4)*

Wynton Marsalis, Jazz at Lincoln Center's music and artistic director, once said, "Music is such a great tool to teach you how to communicate, to teach history, to give you confidence, to just develop your mental capacity and develop your ability to concentrate. Moreover, that's even more true about jazz, since the music requires a longer attention span. It makes you more aware of subtle nuances." (*The Journal News* Jan 25, 2007).

The teachers who had the greatest effect on my life were not necessarily the conservative teachers who played it safe for their security and salary. No, the oddball, unorthodox teachers forced me to think for myself and not to be afraid to stand alone for what I believed. This attitude received reinforcement in my home; my parents encouraged me to never give up.

The one thing these "oddball" teachers had in common was the ability to express themselves clearly and to get their students excited about learning and life.

I firmly believe enthusiasm for their subject and zest for life are the highest qualities a teacher can bring to the classroom. There is nothing worse than a boring teacher!

During the 1940s, we walked to and from school every day without fear of predators or kidnappers. We even walked through the woods to get to Franklin Elementary School, and we never did see a big bad wolf! There were no school buses in our city school district except those used for the sports teams when they traveled. During my elementary school days, we were expected to wear white shirts, dark trousers (no jeans), and shoes (no sneakers). The standards for this public elementary school were quite high.

A family atmosphere permeated the school as parents and teachers had close ties and worked well together. Communication was always clear and present. We were trained during bomb shelter drills to sit under our desks with our hands over our heads (I'm certainly glad that we never faced this reality).

It was a simpler, more defined time, with fewer social distractions and a far smaller number of organized activities. We kept ourselves busy with sports, music, card games, and other simple activities. Imagine a time with no television, iPods, computers, Blackberries, cellphones, bottled water, digital cameras, Kindle, Bluetooth, iCloud, GPS, CDs, DVDs, DVRs, or MP3 players. A school dance, a local concert, or a Saturday afternoon movie was an event to be treasured and talked about for days.

I enjoyed sports and music. I played the saxophone (influenced by my dad, who was a professional saxophonist). I took lessons in school beginning in the fourth grade, and I was soon playing in the school orchestra. By grade six, I had formed my band. Look out, Benny Goodman!

FIRST LIVE PERFORMANCE

Every musician has their first performance, and I was no exception. I attended a public school as well as Catholic Christian Doctrine (CCD classes) at the local Assumption Catholic Church school every Wednesday afternoon. We were dismissed early on Wednesdays so we could attend these dull and dreary classes.

The nuns, who were quite strict and seldom smiled (they must have been weaned on dill pickles and seemed to have a haunting fear that somebody somewhere was happy), decided to host a talent show presented by the students just before Christmas. The recreation hall was brightly decorated, punch and hot cider with cookies were available, and we received a little gift (if we were attentive and applauded during the talent show. I guess "bribery" began at an early age).

I organized some of my musical friends for this gala event, and we diligently rehearsed and prepared the song "America." On the day of the show, our violinist, Donny Annacone, who was the only one who happened to play the melody, was absent from school and unable to perform. We were naturally put off and perplexed about this situation, and I asked Mother Superior what we should do. She said, "You must play. Think of all the hours you spent rehearsing. I'm sure it will sound wonderful."

Well, we played "America" without the melody, and it was terrible. The rest of us had "oom-pah-pah" sounds throughout the piece, and at the time, I was not musically trained enough to realize the melody could be played by another instrument. The nuns were all smiles as we played this non-descript accompaniment to an absent melody. This was my first public appearance—hardly a date to boast about, but memorable. My mom and dad applauded.

Another performance stands out in my mind. While in college at SUNY Potsdam, I served on the Dean's advisory board. Dean Hargrove appointed me to oversee the entertainment for the student assembly programs. Not realizing the seriousness of one in particular where the city mayor, head of the DAR, Red Cross, and Women's League of America were in attendance, I asked my buddy Norm Allison if he would assist me. Together, we decided to begin the assembly program with 6'7" Norm, dressed as a girl dancing the tango with a broom, wearing brown Army boots. Kind of like what Fred Astaire did in one of his movies, only tasteless to the max! Norm is hardly graceful, not a dancer, and he performed a three-minute dance routine like nothing I had ever seen. He danced and wiggled right in front of the staid and proper speakers, who gasped at what they were seeing.

Norm leaped on the stage looking like an oversized Minnie Pearl, while the students roared with laughter. He leaped and pranced all over the stage, taking ungainly giant steps, grunting, and soaring in his brown untied Army boots, to the graceful strains of LeRoy Anderson's "Blue Tango."

The Dean never mentioned it to me, but I noticed that I was soon relieved from my duties as the procurer of entertainment.

The Audition

I always loved the sound of our high school marching band, and I admired the older guys in the band. Bud Treadwell, Bernie Yudowitz, Albert Clementi, and Bobby Renza sure looked like they "had their act together."

At the end of the sixth grade, my dad brought me to the high school at the request of Mr. Shulman, the band director, to audition for the high school marching band. Nobody had ever gotten into the band in grade six before. Most students did not get into the band until grades eight or nine. Mr. Shulman, a soft-spoken, kind, and gentle person, greeted my dad and me as we entered the high school building. He asked me to march up and down the long school hallway while he played drumsticks beating on a wooden chair. He wanted to see if I could step in time with the music and pick my feet up.

Thanks to my dad, I could read music well, and I got a reasonably good sound out of the saxophone. I was thrilled to find out I was accepted into the high school marching band at the end of the sixth grade. Mr. Shulman attempted to fit me with the bright crimson-blue band uniform, but most of them were too large. My mother had to alter the uniform so it would fit me. I was the smallest kid in the band with a big shiny tenor saxophone.

The most exciting experience was when we traveled by bus to away football games. Being the youngest, I was the "darling" of the cheerleaders and band baton twirlers. They thought I was so cute. I had a huge crush on Marie Esposito, the captain of the cheerleaders, and the attention I received was great for my self-esteem.

Love?

A red-haired girl sat by herself a few rows behind me near an open window in seventh-grade English class. I would pretend I was looking out of the window while continuing to get a quick glimpse of this good-looking girl.

Fiona was the love of my life. Her flaming red hair, along with her coy laugh, made her very endearing. During class, I would be distracted by her charm and witty remarks, and I would look for her wherever I went.

After giving Fiona a great deal of thought, I went home and asked my dad if Fiona and I could get married.

His response was measured and full of wisdom, as usual. "I think you ought to first complete the seventh grade and get to the point where you play the saxophone better so you can support a family."

He was right. I'm glad I took his advice. The next week, I fell in love with Angie, a vivacious Italian.

25

Music That Soothes the Savage Beast

One breezy Saturday fall afternoon in 1949, our football team was playing against one of our fiercest rivals, North-Tarrytown High School. The score was tied in the fourth quarter, and during the final thirty seconds of the game, our 6'7" tight end, Jim Cook, jumped high in the end zone and caught a pass from the quarterback George Flood. We won the game! Immediately a riot broke out on the field and in the stands. The players were punching each other; the crowd was screaming, pushing, and shoving in all directions. Mr. Shulman acted quickly and calmly motioned to the band members to remain in our seats. He told us to play our National Anthem. We played it loud and forceful, and by the third time through the piece, the riot stopped. I'm not sure this tactic would garner the same result today, but that day, it was a creative solution and a touch of genius. We were in a state of patriotic bliss. Music certainly did "soothe the savage beast."

We Won

After a winning home football game, the high school band marched from Depew Park through the town and formed a long line while continuing to march. Most of the junior and senior high school students who were not in the band latched on to the end of the line and joined in celebrating with us as we proudly marched and played. Thus, the town folks working in the stores on that Saturday were alerted that the home team won the game. It was a real morale boost for Peekskill.

For many years, on Halloween eve, the high school band, donned in tattered clothes and playing humorous and entertaining music, marched through the town. After the parade, the band went back to the high school where there were dancing and apple dunking contests with cider and doughnuts. It was great fun.

THE STINK I WILL NEVER FORGET!

One year, while we were marching along Washington Street, some junior high kids perched on a high wall overlooking Washington street deliberately threw some dead fish into the bells of the three sousaphones played by my friends Lenny Kaplan, Bob Asheim, and Dave Loshin. The cost to repair the sousaphones paled in comparison to the stink that permeated the band room for weeks. After that experience, I had cloth screens with the school letters on them placed on the bells of each tuba. That was the last Halloween parade in our town, and it was a long time before I ate fish again.

One of the most memorable events for me was when the high school marching band did an evening performance before a capacity crowd at the local minor-league Highlanders baseball stadium. Each band member had a battery-powered light attached to their hats. A simple switch was used to turn the hat lights on or off. We performed the entire halftime show with the stadium lights out, hat lights brightly shining, music memorized, with rotating formations. Show biz at its best!

A BIG STEP

"The mind is not a vessel to be filled, but a fire to be ignited."
- Plutarch

The three years I spent at Drum Hill Jr. High School were exciting and mind-stretching. New friends, new teachers, and changing classes! I was selected to be in a core group during grades seven and eight. Our core group met for three hours each morning, incorporating English, history, and current events. In the afternoon, we traveled to our regular classes, such as art, music, shop, science, math, and physical education.

Mr. Foshay raised his voice over the din of the 24 students in the classroom.

"What did anyone learn yesterday when we visited the mayor's office?"

"I learned that being mayor is not always a job that improves your image and relationship with the public," Mark Jacoby replied after raising his hand.

"Genevieve?" Mr. Foshay nodded and looked to Genevieve Gates.

"I think the mayor's office is drab and needs perking up," she replied, "like putting in rose-colored drapes instead of those morbid brown colors."

"Good observation, Genevieve, but how can changing the drapes and other items affect what he does?" asked Mr. Foshay.

"No girl would feel comfortable in his office," she added. "It's too austere and masculine."

At this point, all the boys in the class let out an audible groan of disapproval.

"Then you believe that the physical surroundings affect how we feel?" remarked Mr. Foshay.

"It certainly does," cried Genevieve as she grasped for a comparison.

"She's a girl," yelled Mark Jacoby, "she can keep the frilly things."

"I see," mused Mr. Foshay.

"I disagree," remarked Bruce Hurt, who needed no coaxing.

"How so?" asked Mr. Foshay.

"Girls like frilly stuff and bright colors and all that stuff," Mark Jacoby blurted out. "It doesn't make any difference to me what his office looks like. Who cares as long as he does his job?"

"Would you feel comfortable negotiating with the mayor if his office were comprised of old cardboard boxes and junk?" Mr. Foshay asserted.

"Are you serious?" replied Bruce. "There had to be a modicum of civility and decorum present that matches the authority of his office."

When the class heard Bruce use the word "modicum," they all oohed and aahed.

Mr. Foshay liked it when we used words not normally a part of our usual vocabulary. He immediately wrote the word "modicum" on the chalkboard, and we had to guess what it meant. If we were stumped, someone would volunteer to look up the word in the huge, red *Webster's Dictionary* prominently displayed on the windowsill.

"We don't eat black bread and drink water," interrupted Genevieve. "We make our food look inviting to the eye. So, the mayor should make his office look inviting for all—and not just for men."

"A good point," resonated Mr. Foshay.

This was the type of prodding for information that went on in our core group. We were encouraged to think, reason, and qualify our remarks. We could also be challenged by the teachers or our fellow students.

The core group integrated students from all ability levels, contained ethnic diversity, and offered a range of religious views. It was a miniature United Nations. We voted on everything, including what grades we should receive based on previously agreed-upon criteria. We took trips to city and county municipal agencies, cultural events, and other thought-provoking activities. Following each experience, we evaluated the event in light of how it benefited our thinking process. The purpose of these trips was to challenge us to think creatively without a prescribed pre-conceived structure. We thrashed out the current events of the day by discussing articles that appeared in *The New York Times*.

“I am not a teacher, but an awakener.”
- Robert Frost

26

SCIENCE?

After lunch, we ambled to Miss Perry's science class. She was a generously proportioned woman, about 250 years old, with a big red nose and troubled gray eyes. She always appeared to have an awful headache. We were concerned about her strange behavior. We often discussed why her nose was so red and decided unanimously (we didn't vote) that Miss Perry must imbibe alcohol to excess.

Our suspicions were confirmed as she often put a shaky hand on the doorknob and entered a closet behind her desk for short periods. Miss Perry soon emerged with her nose seeming to be even redder.

Her breath came thick and hard, her face burning like fire, and her eyes almost snapping out of her head. Poor Miss Perry, she seemed so pathetic and lonesome. Perhaps, Jack Daniels was the only companion she had. She would often enlighten us with facts about animals, such as the following:

- The average housefly lives for one month. (How about the housefly above or below average?)
- A crocodile cannot stick out its tongue. (I'm not going to look!)
- Butterflies taste with their feet.
- Elephants are the only animals that cannot jump.
- A pair of human feet contains 280,000 sweat glands. (Who counted them?)
- Your thumb is the same length as your nose. (Everybody began to check it out)

Learning these facts has certainly shaped my life!

Miss Perry threw a riddle at us one day during a lesson on magnets. "Class, listen carefully to this riddle. My name starts with M, and I pick things up. What am I?"

"A mother!" yelled Ron Chestnut.

Obviously, the answer was a magnet.

We all had a hearty belly laugh at that one while Miss Perry scowled and grunted her disapproval. She never did like Ron.

One cold day in December, Charlie Hunt raised his hand and asked, "What if our knees bent the other way—what would chairs look like?"

The class hooted and howled at the thought while Miss Perry snorted and criticized Charlie for not presenting scientific facts.

After that, Miss Perry smiled and informed us that humans can't lick their elbows. At the end of the class, we all darted into the hall and attempted to lick our elbows. She was right!

I don't remember how much I learned about science from Miss Perry, but we did learn a lot about Miss Perry.

THE PRINCIPAL OF THE THING

Our principal was Mr. Donnelly, who never ceased to astonish us with his ability to manipulate numbers. We would repeatedly go into his office to challenge him by presenting him with columns of numbers to add. On occasion, we would present Mr. Donnelly with eight or nine rows of numbers deep with ten numbers across. Amazingly, he would take his right hand, place it at the top of the rows of numbers, and slowly glide his hand down the long column of numbers. When his right hand reached the bottom of the numbers, he would pick up a pen and write down the answer as quickly as that! The incredible thing was that his answers were always accurate. I was having trouble in math, and he could easily plow through ten rows of numbers with apparent ease.

It wasn't fair!

MY SECOND PUBLIC APPEARANCE

As student president of the Jr. High School, I was asked by the faculty to present a short speech at graduation. My topic was "How to Be Successful in High School." I was seated next to Mr. Donnelly, the principal, the superintendent of schools, the mayor of Peekskill, and other administrators and teachers. In front of me was the lectern holding a microphone. Next to the lectern was a table with 225 diplomas neatly rolled up and piled high with a dark blue ribbon around each. When it was my turn to speak, I was introduced and accompanied by audience applause. On my way to the microphone, I accidentally bumped into the table and all 225 diplomas rolled off into the orchestra pit. I was mortified. I wanted to crawl under the table and die! My second public appearance was even worse than the Catholic school talent show. At that moment, I felt that life was soup and I was a fork!

27

New Settings

"An artist is always out of step with the time. He has to be."
- Orson Wells

Upon graduation from grade nine, I entered Peekskill High School, where I was thrilled about the new challenges and opportunities that lay ahead.

My six years in the high school marching band were exciting times. I never missed a practice, parade, or football game during that time. I even began designing the half-time shows for the marching band, working closely with Mr. Shulman.

My life was blessed when the Board of Education gave me a grant so I could attend the State University of New York at Potsdam: Crane School of Music. Without their generosity, my parents could have never sent me to college.

I formed a dance band in grade six, which I continued through grades seven to nine. My dad was a professional bandleader, so I learned a lot about organizing and operating a band from him. My four-piece band in high school consisted of me on tenor saxophone, trumpeter Johnny Allen, pianist Dolores Spotswood, and Bootsie

Tinsley or Freddie Wilkins on the drums. We often played during lunch hours. We played at least once per week as the students danced to the latest popular music.

THE BIG APPLE

During a local talent show at the Paramount Theatre, our band won the top prize of $50. My dad recommended said we needed a gimmick to edge out the competition. "Try kneeling on one knee and play the sax solo behind your back!"

So, in the middle of our song, I daringly and unexpectedly dropped to my right knee, thrust the tenor saxophone behind my back, and played a bluesy rocking solo. This caused uproar and brought the house down. Playing behind my back is easy to do. The saxophone fingering is the same, and the hands remain in the same position, but the audience ate it up.

Because we won, we were invited to audition for the Ted Mack Amateur hour in New York City the following week. When our time came to audition, we took our places with our instruments. Although nervous, I again did my routine with my sax behind my back, and I thought we sounded good that day.

A tall man wearing a tan raincoat and a fedora approached us after we performed. "I'm Norby Walters, and I'm a music talent agent. You sounded great, and I would like to book you in a club in Harlem beginning in two weeks."

We were astonished. Johnny and Bootsie jumped at the opportunity and yelled, "We'll take the gig."

I said, "Thank you, Mr. Walters, but I'm only 16, and I have to finish high school and go to college next year."

Dolores said the same thing. Then Norby screamed at us, "If you don't take this, I'll ban you from every club in New York for the rest of your lives!

Wow! Our first time in New York, and we had just been banned from playing there again. We couldn't believe our ears!

Then a representative from the Ted Mack Show approached me and my uncle and asked if we could come into his office. "The band sounded good, but we can't use a mixed band on television."

"Is that because we have a girl in our band?" I asked.

He replied, "No, because there are coloreds in your band."

I was quite surprised to hear this. After all, my dad told me that Benny Goodman had a mixed band in 1938, but I guess the Ted Mack folks were not ready to take such a step forward.

I never did tell the other band members why we were not selected. Recently, however, after many years, I received a telephone call from Dolores, our pianist. When I told her why we didn't get the chance to perform on The Ted Mack Show, she said, "I kind of had a feeling that was the reason."

My uncle Nick verbally blasted the producer for his prejudice and small-mindedness. The man shrugged his shoulders and left.

Times have changed, but during the early 1950s, my parents always taught me to judge others by their character and musical ability and not by their appearance.

PREJUDICE HURTS!

Broadway composer Richard Rodgers wrote a song called "You've Got to be Carefully Taught" in the 1949 musical *South Pacific*. It is about prejudice against those who look differently. The producers of the show wanted Rodgers to remove the song from the show. Rodgers replied that if the song was removed, he would close down the show. The song stayed in.

A clear account of color prejudice happened when my fellow teacher Tom Readyoff was teaching an orchestra class at Drum Hill Middle School. There were two eighth-grade girls in the orchestra, one playing flute and the other cello. The flutist Mary Ann was 75 percent blind, and her sister Florence, who played cello, was totally blind. They were born this way due to a mistake by a doctor. Both girls were excellent players. Mary Ann, the flutist, could read music if she was very close to the music stand. Florence, the cellist, had an amazing memory and could listen to a piece once and play it perfectly the second time.

Reggie, a Black kid, who liked to poke fun at others, played the cello and sat next to Florence. After the orchestra finished a selection, Florence began screaming and crying hysterically.

Tom Readyoff calmed her and asked why she was so upset. In tears, she replied, "Reggie told me I was Black!"

The silence stunned everybody except Reggie, who thought it was amusing. No doubt Florence's parents trained her to think in this way. Yes, "You've Got to be Carefully Taught."

Who Has Musical Ears?

Three of my buddies, Tony Salvatori on bass trombone, Pete Yellin on alto saxophone, and Lloyd Michaels on lead trumpet, were playing with the Buddy Rich Band. They wanted me to go with Buddy's big band to Japan, but it would mean leaving my teaching job and my wife and two kids. So, I asked, "Can I play during the summers?" But that wouldn't work.

I was invited to come to a recording session of Buddy's band for his big band album, *West Side Story*. I found out that Buddy did not read music but had an amazing ear and memory.

My first impression was that nobody spoke until Buddy did, and nobody gave an opinion unless Buddy asked for one. I sat in the control room behind Buddy, who was seated at the console. I listened to a "take" and said to myself, "The bari sax is too loud."

Within two seconds, Buddy announced, "The bari has to come down."

After another take, I said to myself, "I think Lloyd is a bit sharp on the lead trumpet part."

Immediately Buddy chimed in, "Let's do the last section again. Lloyd was a bit high on that one."

I admired Buddy's ear for discerning musical sounds and his musical memory.

A few months later, I was invited to bring one of my arrangements to one of Buddy's band rehearsals. I went to a New York City studio, and Buddy entered wearing a Dracula shirt doing arm exercises as we walked. What a sight to see!

Another arranger brought in an arrangement of a classical song for a jazz band. Buddy hated it. "We don't play this stuff," he screamed with a little more colorful language added in and threw his drumsticks at the guy. The poor guy ducked, and Buddy threw the guy out of the studio.

To say I was nervous is an understatement. I walked over in front of the band. He looked at me and said, "Kid, I don't read music, so you lift one finger if I have a one-measure solo, two fingers for a two-measure solo, and you better not cut me off late!"

"Okay, Buddy, I got it."

The band played the arrangement, and there was silence.

Buddy finally said, "Let's do it again." So, we played it again as I conducted the band.

After they played it the second time, Buddy said nothing, and they took a break. I was sure that my first impression as an arranger for Buddy Rich was a disaster. Buddy saw me in the hall and said, "Hey, kid, I like that chart! How much?"

I replied, "$400."

He said, "Good, leave the chart with me, and I'll send you the bucks."

I replied that my music attorney (actually my friends in the band) told me, "Never give an arrangement to anyone without getting the money upfront."

Buddy looked at me and said," Whatever," and walked away.

I never got paid.

NEVER SAY NO!

When I was in my late twenties, I began studying music in New York City with top composers and arrangers, Bernard Wagenaar from the Julliard School of Music and jazz composer Jimmy Giuffre. During this time, I met John Krance, who was one of the best music arrangers in New York City. He gave excellent advice, which I have never forgotten. "Vince, learn all you can about every style of music. Analyze scores and listen to the best music. When your skills have developed, never say 'no' to any music assignment offered to you. If you say 'no,' you will never be asked again. Even if you have to 'bone up' on a style, do it quickly, but never refuse an assignment. You have to be good, and you have to be fast. Most clients take their time deciding on a project and then are in a hurry to get it completed."

I have been able to take many great assignments over the years and one, in particular, placed me in an interesting situation. I was music director for the annual Thanksgiving parade in Philadelphia for ten years. For one week in October, I traveled to Philadelphia to record choirs and professional musicians in a recording studio. I was responsible for all music prerecorded for the parade for dancers, vocalists, and so on.

During one of the assignments, my producer scheduled the song "Hey, Look Me Over" for the choir. I received a phone call one afternoon from the producer. "Vince, regarding the song 'Hey, Look Me Over,' can you change the words to include the word 'Philadelphia' six times and have most of the names of the band instruments mentioned in the song? And I need the lyrics on my desk by 11 o'clock tomorrow morning."

I naturally said, "Yes," with a massive surge of energy. I stayed up most of the night completing the assignment and sent an email copy of the lyrics to the producer the next morning.

At my rehearsal band in New York City, often musicians would come by and listen. After one rehearsal, a man approached me. "Hi, my name is Richard Lavsky. I own a recording studio in New York City and need someone who can orchestrate a movie. Can you do this?"

Remembering what John Krance told me, I immediately responded, "Sure, I would love to do it for you." I gave him my business card.

"Great, I will contact you."

A few weeks went by, and I had forgotten about my meeting with Richard. I knew that talk was cheap, and sometimes things are said just to impress others.

One Friday night, I received a phone call. It was Richard Lavsky.

"Vince, I need you to arrange music for a movie. I wrote the themes and the timings, and you will need to orchestrate them for a 65-piece orchestra. Can you come to New York City at a music prep studio around 4 p.m. Wednesday to view a screening of the movie?"

I immediately said I would be there and thanked him for the project.

My background was thorough in orchestrating for an orchestra, but scoring a movie was another thing altogether. So, I went to the local library the next day and took out all the movie books they had. I owned film-scoring books by Frank Skinner and Earl Hagen, which I never had the time to read. I devoured the information over the next few days and memorized all the needed terminology I would need to carry on an intelligent discussion with movie folks.

The movie was *Brighty of the Grand Canyon,* starring Joseph Cotton and Dick Foran.

The day for the recording came…I became quite nervous after I realized who some of the musicians were in the orchestra, such as the first clarinetist for the New York Philharmonic, Joe Wilder, a top jazz trumpet player, and many others. My thoughts ran wild. "Perhaps I didn't transpose the French Horn part correctly?" "What will these great musicians think of my arranging?" "If my scoring doesn't sound well, will I ever get another music gig in New York City?"

Richard conducted the sessions, and I sat behind him with the scores in the event any notes had to change. When I heard the opening trills in the woodwinds and the French horn lines ascending, I knew all would be well. Finally, peace entered my soul.

Since that time, Richard and I have become great friends, and he has hired me for numerous recording dates. Richard and I have the same "wacky" humor, and no doubt this was a plus in establishing our close relationship. One time Richard told me he was working on a musical, *Emperor Norton,* with the well-known radio personality Gene Klavan and asked me to orchestrate the music for a 26-piece orchestra. After I completed the project, Richard recorded all the parts for the musical on his Synclavier, a sophisticated music recording device that duplicates the sound of a real orchestra. He used real vocalists to record on top of my orchestrations, and the result was amazing to hear. Unfortunately, like most musicals, it was not picked up by producers, despite the great music and interesting story.

Another assignment Richard gave me was to arrange the ABC News Theme for the Peter Jennings show. This was great fun, and I had the opportunity to conduct "world-class" musicians such as Lou Soloff (trumpet with the group Blood, Sweat, and Tears) and drummer Steve Gadd (who performed with Steely Dan, Paul Desmond, Chet Baker, and Chick Corea, among others).

I realized that to score movies for a living, it was best if one lived near Hollywood. My friend, Dave Loshin, moved from Peekskill, New York to Los Angeles. He heard about the "Brightly" project and asked if I would consider moving to L.A. to compose movies. He said that his brother Michael was an attorney and some of his clients were movie producers, and I could easily get work in L.A. I had a good teaching job at Peekskill High School and had a wife and three children to consider, so I respectfully declined the offer. But I did compose and conduct some movies for Regent University in Norfolk, Virginia later on and studied film scoring in New York City with Don Sebesky.

STACKING THE DECK

I was hired to score two commercials and they were to be recorded in New York City. The first was for Colgate toothpaste. I found that working with non-musical producers can offer challenges that demand ingenuity and finesse.

The first producer told me in the pre-session talks that he wanted the music to sound "macho." I thought, "How does one produce a macho sound? Timpani? Brass instruments?" I told him I could do that, not knowing exactly what he meant.

On the day of the recording session, I had timpani, brass, and a rhythm section ready to record. Before I began, I stopped the assistant engineer, Jay, and asked if he would occasionally pop his head into the recording booth and exclaim, "Boy, does that sound macho!" Jay agreed. He did just that about three times, and the producer smiled and loved the session.

Aah! The power of music coupled with the power of suggestion!

The second session was for strings, three French horns, and a few woodwinds. When we met with the two producers, one asked if I could include a tenor saxophone in the recording. I had not planned to use the tenor sax or any sax due to its fullness of sound...it just didn't seem to fit with my concept for the commercial. So, I asked a friend to bring his tenor saxophone to the session. I gave him a simple part (whole notes and half notes) and told him to play very softly during the session. He did exactly as I asked. The producer was delighted that I included the sax in the recording. However, in the final mixdown, we lowered the volume of the tenor sax dramatically. Sometimes one has to protect his musical ideas by fortifying verbal and visual ones.

ANOTHER ENCOUNTER WITH PROS

I was blessed to have great friends in the Army with me who played with the top big jazz bands at that time. Jerry Puleo was a wonderful friend and trumpet player who organized a big band of 18 professional musicians. We rehearsed every Tuesday night at Marshall Brown's Studio on 72nd Street in New York City. Some of the pros who were in the band were:

Trumpets: Jerry Puleo, Tommy Sullivan, Danny Styles; Bobby Helms, Clyde Resinger.

Trombones: Wayne Andre, Billy Watrous, Alan Raph, Tony Salvatori, Myron Yules, Joe Lane, and Billy Verplanck.

Saxophones: Pete Yellin (alto)), Bobby Porcelli (alto), Paul Rotante (alto), Joe Melitti (tenor), Buz Brauner (tenor), Gene Allen (baritone sax).

Rhythm Section: Johnny Morris (piano), Gene Bertoncini and Jay Berliner (guitars), Norman Edge and George Duvivier (bass), Tommy Vig and Mike Manieri (vibes), Mel Dworkin and Stu Martin (drums), and many others.

The musicians even chipped in two dollars for every rehearsal so I could pay the cost of using the rehearsal studio. We rehearsed every Tuesday night for a few years.

In the studio next to us, the Gerry Mulligan band was rehearsing for one month for three hours before our rehearsal. So, I arrived early to listen to that great big band and watched and listened to what Gerry told them. He, like Buddy Rich, was very particular about what he expected from the musicians, and I picked up lots of helpful ideas from both of them.

After the rehearsal, I would go for coffee with the great jazz trumpeter Conte Candoli, who played the jazz chair in Gerry's band. We became friends and he taught me a lot about running a rehearsal. "Always begin a rehearsal with an easy, relaxed piece so the guys can get in a groove., and the rest of the rehearsal will be easy." I always remembered that and applied it to every group I conducted.

MY DAD, THE BOXER

My dad, a strong, quiet man, exhibited lots of wisdom about things and people.

When I was about ten years old, he would periodically ask me to listen to the radio with him as he listened to broadcasts of professional boxing matches. His favorite fighters were Joe Louis, Sugar Ray Robinson, Jake La Motta, Billy Conn, Tony Zale, Rocky Graziano, and Jersey Joe Walcott.

Boxing was at the bottom of my interest list, but I didn't want to disappoint my dad. I noticed he would get excited during each match when a certain fighter threw a good punch or knocked his opponent down.

Many years later, after my dad passed away at 90 years old, I asked my mom about his interest in boxing. "Why boxing? I thought he was only involved in music?"

My mom replied, "I guess he never told you about his experiences with boxing as a young man?"

"No, he never told me anything."

"Your dad lived with his family in Beacon, New York, where Melio Bettina, the light heavyweight champion of the world, trained for his matches. He volunteered to be Melio's sparring partner."

"And they let him do that?" I said in astonishment.

"Yes," she replied. "He did it for one year, and they paid him one dollar per round. I'm glad his mother never found out about it; she would have been furious!"

I wish I knew this while my dad was alive. I would have asked where he learned to box and, "Pop, did you ever land a punch that sent him across the ring?" My dad and Melio Bettina were about the same size at 5'9" and 160 lbs.

My dad could do many things that I would never attempt. He could fix anything in the house, could cut his own hair, was proficient on the saxophone, guitar, and trombone, and he was a great jazz drummer.

I CAN'T DO THAT!

When my mom and dad got married, he was playing drums in a five-piece band in Cold Spring, New York, at a jazz club in 1933. One evening, a man approached my dad during a break and told him that a famous professional trumpet player "drying out" from alcoholism was at the nearby sanatorium. He asked my dad if he could sit in with his band on weekends. He also asked if he would keep him away from the bar. My dad didn't drink and said he would do that.

That following Friday evening, the man entered the club with another man carrying a trumpet case. The man carrying the trumpet case said, "Hi Nick, I'm Red Nichols."

My father said you could have knocked Red over with a feather. This was the famous Red Nichols, leader of the "Five Pennies." (Years later, I saw the film with Danny Kaye playing the part of Red Nichols). My dad said that Red was the smoothest trumpet player he ever heard. Such melodic and pretty sounds came out of his horn.

He kept Red away from alcohol for that year, and Red liked my dad's drumming, so he offered him a position in his band. My dad turned it down since he was married and had a new baby at home. Red said he was disappointed, but that he understood the situation.

A friend of my dad's who played saxophone with the big bands in the 1920s and 1930s, Joe Davis, informed him that Tony Pastor (bandleader and tenor sax player) was looking for a drummer. Joe suggested that he audition for his big band. Joe called Tony Pastor and set the date for my dad to come to New York City to audition.

My dad walked to the train wearing a bright red sweater, with his drumsticks under his arm, and ventured to the Hotel Lincoln for his audition.

When he walked through the door of the club, Tony Pastor greeted him with a big smile. "Hello Nick, welcome to my band. Go sit with the drums."

My dad immediately tuned each drum to his specifications. He gave the drum part to Tony and asked if he could have a copy of the first trumpet part. He said he can "kick" the band better using the trumpet part. "Kick" means setting up the brass figures with drum fills before their entrance. The band liked my dad's playing.

Tony asked him to join the band, and my dad said he would when they played in New York City. Tony looked disappointed and told him they were a traveling band that played in New York City a few times a year. He told my dad he would be glad to set up an audition for him with the Paul Whiteman Orchestra, which performed mostly in New York City. My dad thanked Tony and took the train home.

My dad felt that playing while "on the road" would disrupt his family, and the temptations for alcohol, drugs, and other things would be problematic.

Thirty years after my dad lost two of his fingers, he was at the peak of his musical career playing the alto saxophone. Besides being proficient in the drums, saxophone, and clarinet, he also taught himself how to play guitar and trombone. It was amazing he could learn any instrument without taking lessons, just by listening to recordings and reading music books.

At that time, I had an 18-piece big band that rehearsed at the Vagabond House near Peekskill, New York. One particular Sunday, I combined the best musicians from our area with about seven musicians that came up from New York City.

My dad was playing the lead alto saxophone part with the band, and sitting next to him was a tenor saxophone player who just got off of the Woody Herman Big Band. At the break, the tenor sax player from Woody's band said, "Vince, I don't believe it! Your dad has only two fingers on his right hand, and I have all five. He plays as good as I do."

I told him I didn't understand how he did it either.

MEANSPIRITED

The students were pouring down the hall with their sheaves of notebooks in their hands. We entered the noisy and somewhat dirty shop area, the domain of Mr. Shockton. Mr. Shockton was a rough-edged kind of person who would verbally abuse and occasionally slap students around if they didn't quickly understand what he was teaching. He said it was for their good. We considered him a loud-mouthed person with mule's ears. He was externally impatient as if haunted by a fear that he would fall short of his self-made goal. I had practically no talent or interest in metal shop work. Working with metal for me, was sort of like teaching an Eskimo how to skydive.

One day, during metal shop class, I was having great difficulty understanding how to take a project apart. I leaned over to Charlie Hunt and asked if he could solve the situation for me. I couldn't make hide-nor-hair of what Mr. Shockton was talking about.

Of course, there was skill involved with working with metal, and I had none. Therefore, acting under the coaxing of Charlie Hunt, I began disassembling the metal unit beginning at the top. Mr. Shockton hesitated, but only for a moment, and said, "Corozine, can't you understand anything about metalworking?'

"It's not so easy for me," I replied. "The only metal I've ever worked with is my saxophone."

He considered that an impertinent answer, and he tapped my head with a steel bolt, saying, "Perhaps someday you'll understand how to put things together." Well, I never did understand how to put metal objects together, but I did learn how to put music notes together.

When I came home, my dad took one look at my forehead and asked what happened. I told him. He rushed with me to the school to confront Mr. Shockton. My dad was a strong, quiet, unassuming person who seldom got angry. He had a solid build, and his strength was impressive. The principal, Mr. Frisch, intervened just in time. My dad was spared a jail sentence for assault, and I was spared the embarrassment.

That was the last time Mr. Shockton ever laid a hand on me.

FAMILY TREE

I've often wondered about my grandparents and from where in Italy they came. One day I asked my dad, "Where did the name 'Corozine' come from?"

"When your grandparents came over from Italy," he said, "they were in line at Ellis Island with lots of other immigrants.

"That was a long time ago," I said.

"Yeah, in the 1920s," he replied. "When your grandfather was asked his name, he said, 'Vincenzo Carrazzini.'"

"So that's our real name?"

"It was," he said until the officials couldn't spell it and wrote 'Corozine' instead."

"Wow, so that's how we got our name."

"And Aunt Kate," he said, "her real name is 'Archangela.'"

"That's a great name, Pop!"

"Well, they couldn't spell that either," he said, "and they wrote Kate."

"I wonder how many others went through this loss of identity."

"And your other grandfather Sabato had his name changed to Samuel."

"But that's not even close," I sputtered. "However, both names do begin with an "s."

I guess my relatives thought that to be an American, they had to conform to this treatment.

"Pop?" I asked, "what does our name mean in Italian?"

"Carrozza means large carriage, and Carazzini means little carriage," he said.

"How did we get that name?" I inquired.

"Either your grandfather-built carriages—or stole them or fell off of one," he chuckled.

I thought, "That was a typical response from my dad."

MY FAMILY

My Italian family: lots of great food, fun, and a close, loving family. My dad was a professional saxophone player, while my mom was a great cook and loved everybody with a hug and a kiss. While at college, anticipating going home for Easter break, I phoned my parents and asked my mom if I could bring a few of my friends home for Easter break for three to four days.

She excitedly said, "Yes, we would love to meet them." Well, I showed up with my whole jazz band of thirteen guys. She loved all over them and cooked for them, and my dad had rehearsals for three days in our living room with them. They all brought their instruments.

We always had musicians in our home at 335 Smith Street in Peekskill, New York, and the neighbors enjoyed listening to us play. One night during the summer, my dad was holding a rehearsal of his 8-piece band at our home as usual on a Thursday night and all the neighbors sat on their porches drinking their beer or wine while listening to us play.

One day Jimmy Masculino, our neighbor across the street was speaking to my dad. He said, "Hey Nicka, How a come you no finisha the piece that you playa?"

My dad explained that it was a rehearsal, and when we play a gig, we play the whole song.

Jimmy nodded and said, "That'sa good idea, Nicka.

I began playing the saxophone when I was eight years old. My dad taught me to read music (by subdividing the rhythmic beats), and I became a good reader. I wanted to play just like him.

PAY ATTENTION TO MOM

My mom was a loving, caring mother who seldom raised her voice. Whenever she would address me as "Vincent!" I knew I did something wrong, like not hanging up my clothes or leaving my books all over the living room floor. However, I remember her exploding in anger at my younger brother Richie. She came home after purchasing a brand-new pair of white sneakers for Richie. I think Richie was in middle school. He walked outside into the yard and smudged brown mud on the shoes.

My brother is now a talented visual artist, and no doubt carefully considered the matter and concluded that the white shoes need a bit of contrast.

My mother screamed at him and ranted and raved about how much the sneakers cost. "Why would you do that to a nice pair of sneakers?"

Richie just looked at her in amazement and shrugged his shoulders. That was the only time I ever saw my mother get angry.

DISASTER STRIKES!

At the age of thirty, my dad lost three fingers on his right hand in an industrial accident. He played in a band on weekends and worked at an oil cloth factory during the weekdays. Something was stuck in the machine, and he tried to grab it...they couldn't reattach his fingers!

I remember my mom answering the phone on a small brown wooden table and saying, "Dad's been hurt! Dad's been hurt," and crying.

I was five years old and my brother Nick was three. We didn't understand what that meant...did he hurt his shoulder or his toe?

My dad was never one to grumble or complain in any way. He was always cheerful and worked very hard at what he did. While in the hospital, my dad began drawing sketches with his left hand. He was an excellent clarinet player (like Woody Herman) and a great sax player (like Marshall Royal and Johnny Hodges). He was diagramming keys to be added to his clarinet so the lower three notes could be played by the right pinky finger. It was an ingenious idea. A famous woodwind repair technician told me after seeing his clarinet, that he had never seen anything like it. My dad returned to playing professionally after only three months! Vision, commitment, not accepting defeat, and smiling all the way. That was my dad!

A Composer is Born

On a cloudy Saturday afternoon in April, my dad and I were walking along Highway 9 in Peekskill. My dad was taking me to Augie Salerno's Barbershop to get a haircut. We couldn't afford a car, and walking was the only way to get anywhere. I looked up at my dad and asked, "Pop, you and I play the sax, but when I listen to your records, I hear saxes, trumpets, trombones, and the rhythm section playing different things. Like with Benny Goodman, Les Brown, Count Basie, and Duke Ellington bands. How do they put all that music together?"

"I can teach you how to play the sax, read music, improvise jazz, and play lead alto with authority, but I can't teach you how to arrange music. If you want to know, you will have to study with the best composers."

My dad, a self-taught professional saxophone player, didn't have the musical education I had, but he had marvelous instincts regarding music.

Later in life, during a Thanksgiving vacation from college, I brought home a cassette of Beethoven's 7th Symphony. I asked my dad to listen to one movement of the symphony and tell me his opinion.

"He is a good composer," my dad offered upon listening.

I asked him why he said that. "Because you think the music is going one way, and it surprises us by going in another direction. It is not predictable."

"Predictable." That word stuck in my mind. Years later, following my stint in the U.S. Army at West Point, I began studying music composition with Jimmy Giuffre, who asked me to bring him a piece of music I arranged.

He listened and remarked, "You have a good grasp of writing for instruments, but your music is too damn predictable!"

Ouch! The word "predictable" resonated within my soul like a cannon shot through a tunnel.

"What can I do about it?" I asked him.

"Study free counterpoint with me," he replied.

I did, and he changed how I constructed music and altered my approach to musical composition.

During my college days, I met a fellow student, Ted Spillman. Ted was a trumpet major who knew how to arrange music. He studied with Robert Farnon in Canada. Ted and I would have lunch, and he would show me how to voice (distribute) the instruments in the jazz band. In exchange for this, I would sing or play musical lines for Ted, and he would write them down and complete a musical arrangement. Occasionally Ted would say, "No, don't ever put the root of a dominant seventh chord in the saxes or other instruments. Use the chord ninth instead." I asked why. He remarked, "It is very square, like the Guy Lombardo band...don't ever do it."

After my time studying with Ted and my numerous arrangements for the Varsity Jazz Band of which I was a member, I went on to study 16th and 18th-century counterpoint with Charles Walton at Columbia University, composition with Bernard Wagenaar of the Juilliard School of Music, and film scoring with Don Sebesky. However, my studies with Jimmy Giuffre changed the way I *think* about music, and for this, I am eternally grateful.

How I Met-a You Mother

My dad often told me the story of how he met my mom. My mom was a beautiful, slim Italian girl called Carmella Spiotti. When she was sixteen, she asked her father if she could go to the dance at the Knights of Columbus Hall. He said, "No, Carmella, you are too younga."

My mom stamped her foot. "Pop, if you let me go to the dance, I promise this will be the last dance I ever go to.

Her father again said, "No Carmella, too younga, too younga."

Carmella's sister, my aunt Anne went up to their father and whispered something in his ear. "Okay Carmella, you can go if your sisters Anne and Katie go with you to watcha you."

My mother wondered what her sister Anne said to her father and asked her.

Anne replied, "I told Pop that if you don't let her go, we will never cook pasta for him again!" They all laughed about that.

My mother went to the dance, and my dad was playing drums with a five-piece band. My mom thought he was so handsome, and my dad noticed her as well.

He was four years older than my mom at twenty years old, and they went out for about two years before they got married. But her father Sam insisted that when she went out, she had to take her friend Emma Acquillio with them. After about two years of dating (with Emma always along), my dad told me he wasn't sure if he was supposed to marry my mom or Emma!

Watch Your Manners!

My uncle Nick, my mom's brother, was a great mechanic and a dedicated poker gambler. My aunt Anne enrolled in the teaching program at New York University. When my uncle Nick won at poker each week, he would come home and put some money on the dining table and tell my aunt Anne, "Here is your tuition and travel money for the next month." He put my aunt Anne through four years at NYU.

My Aunt Anne became an English and Latin teacher, and whenever she visited us, she would always correct our English. "Now, Vincent, you should say, 'may I,' and not can I.'"

I knew she was right, but my brothers Nick and Richie would wince in pain at the mention of her name. She was proper in all her ways.

While I was away at college at SUNY Potsdam getting my degree in music, my aunt Anne sent me a large package filled with delicious-looking homemade chocolate chip cookies, and she put popped popcorn in the box to keep the cookies from breaking up.

The guys in my fraternity gobbled them up in three minutes. With my sense of humor, I sent a letter to my aunt Anne thanking her for the popcorn. My mom called and told me that my aunt Anne didn't think that was funny and expected a written apology. I did write her and apologized. I found out later that my dad thought it was amusing.

My uncle Nick knew how to work with others. After he left his job as a mechanic, he and my aunt Helen opened a restaurant in Peekskill. He told me that if you want customers to return, give them something for free. So, he posted a sign saying, "Your second cup of coffee is free!" He told me that lots of folks returned to get the second coffee, and business was booming!

To Be Or Not To Be...

"Teachers open the door…you enter by yourself."
- Anonymous

During my junior year in high school, our English teacher was quickly skimming through papers on his desk. Mr. Mendel was a small, diminutive, slightly balding man with a curious sense of introspection about life. He had a sneaky way of moving around the room, but what I noticed most were his eyes. They had a queer trick of focusing inward at times. Whenever he was asked a question, he would reflect for a moment and then lean forward with what he considered an expression of great shrewdness.

Mr. Mendel taught English with a poetic flair and emphasis. He read to us frequently from *The Rubaiyat of Omar Khayyam*. He was sometimes inclined to see the darker side of life. His peculiar mannerisms made him somewhat of a social oddball. He was almost timid and withdrawn to the point of wanting to hide from view when in the presence of others. He frequently quoted famous writers, and amused himself by sneaking in material that was, in my opinion, "off the wall."

Mr. Mendel always seemed to be reading and studying during lunch, study hall, and even during hall duty. "Mr. Mendel," I asked, "what keeps you studying? You're so smart already."

He looked up and said, "I would rather have my students drink from a running stream than a stagnant pool."

Mr. Mendel knew how to keep us interested during the mundane poetry reading and classic stories we studied in class. Something mysterious and wonderful things happened when he read poetry. His passionate interest in poetry, books, and drama was infectious. There was just enough dramatic flamboyance in his presentations to arouse our curiosity.

Gary Larsen cut English class often, and eventually, Mr. Mendel told him, "Gary, you're not flunking English class, but I will give you another year in which to get to know you better."

Such a poetic way of presenting bad news.

However, he was the classic "hen-pecked" husband with an overbearing wife who dominated him. I think he was terrified of her. I learned from Mr. Mendel not to accept everything for its face value but to be willing to challenge all assumptions made. He was also the drama coach and produced some rather progressive plays for that time. Mr. Mendel felt safe in the classroom reading his poetry with flamboyance and directing dramatic shows. Life at school must have been far better for him than life at home.

One time he ended the class by saying, "What I need is a list of specific unknown problems we will encounter." There is no doubt in my mind that Mr. Mendel walks clockwise.

28

Not a Babe Ruth!

I could throw out a runner at home plate from anywhere in the outfield at Depew Park. If I could, I would have played outfield for both teams and never come to bat.

I was an avid New York Giant fan—Bobby Thompson was my hero—while my brother Nick rooted for the Brooklyn Dodgers. We were constantly clashing over which team was the best. Both of us played varsity baseball, and I have to admit Nick was a better player than I.

During my senior year in high school, eight of us from the varsity baseball team ventured to Yonkers, New York, to try out for a major league baseball team, the St. Louis Browns. When I arrived, they slapped number 37 on my back and told me to get into the outfield. A great start for me, as I was confident and comfortable there. They hit the ball to me for a full five minutes. I caught every ball and quickly returned the ball by throwing hard strikes to the plate on one bounce. They were impressed.

"Number 37, if you can hit half as well as you can field, we'll take you," a coach remarked.

At this point, my spirits began to flag. I was seriously debating whether this could be the fulfillment of my boyhood dreams. Suddenly, reality began to rise within me. I stood in line, waiting to bat, behind huge players from Scarsdale, Mt. Vernon, White Plains, and Yonkers. Bigger schools with bigger baseball players. They had enormous necks, heavily built frames, and massive arms. I weighed in at about 155 pounds (soaking wet) and lacked the power to hit the ball a long distance. I watched these mammoth players blast the ball into the outfield stands.

With my knees trembling slightly, I hit a harmless grounder to shortstop, dribbled risk-free back to the pitcher, and warily hit one to second base. With the 12-15 swings I mustered, I never did hit the ball out of the infield. Things progressed in this way for about three minutes, and then I happened to direct my attention to the coach walking toward me.

"Number 37," he said, "what else do you do for a living?"

"I'm a musician," I replied.

He patted me on the back and said, "Great, that's what you should do."

Was I shattered? No, I just accepted the reality that sports would be an avocation for me and not a way to make a living.

Later when I attended college, I was asked to try out for the baseball team. The coach watched me and said the same thing the professional coach said, "If you can hit half as well as you play the outfield…"

I knew what was coming next.

He watched me hit and asked if anybody ever told me that I move my head before I swing, causing me to swing late. What a revelation! I didn't play baseball in college due to a scheduling conflict with my musical organizations. However, I am pleased to say that when I played fast-pitch softball years later, I didn't move my head and hit the ball quite well.

IT'S NOT PICASSO!

Mr. Kennelworth was an eccentric, sarcastic man. From the moment he came into the room, he continually eyeballed the pretty young girls. He had a caustic sense of humor and a nasty, irritating cough. His favorite pastime was relentlessly teasing the young girls.

His teaching about art was conventional and sometimes a bit tedious, but his lifestyle and mannerisms were most fascinating to observe.

There were times in class when Mr. Kennelworth expected us to sketch from observing a basket of fruit, or we would go out of doors and sketch some scenery. One time he posed with a pair of blue earmuffs over his ears and asked us to draw him. Absurd? Certainly! He wasn't amused when I drew a cuckoo bird above his head. I'm sure Mr. Kennelworth walked in a clockwise motion.

"I like to paint dairy cows," muttered Harry Strum, a jock who showed little or no interest in artistic things.

"Did you grow up on a dairy farm?" Mr. Kennelworth asked.

"No, but I watch lots of cartoons with cows in them."

"Don't the cows on television look different than those in real life?" commented Mr. Kennelworth.

"Maybe, but who would know the difference anyway?"

"I certainly would," said Mr. Kennelworth with a bit of ridicule.

"Were you ever a dairy farmer?" asked Harry.

"No, but I've seen real cows on a farm," replied Mr. Kennelworth.

Harry responded, “Do my cows have to look like real cows? Is that important?”

“Most people would like it if they did look like cows,” replied Mr. Kennelworth.

“Why can’t I just take a photograph of a cow to please these people? Don’t you think?”

“Are you telling me what is and what is not good art?” A wild, frenzied look came over his face.

“I could never do that; it all looks the same to me!” replied Harry.

“Do you expect to pass this course, young man?” stammered Mr. Kennelworth.

“Yes, if I can find a cow to draw.”

On another warm day in April, Mr. Kennelworth asked Harry, “Do you see that girl standing by the window?”

“Yes, that pretty girl in a pink dress,” was his reply.

“Is that all you see?” exclaimed Mr. Kennelworth.

“No, she appears to eat too much and will be fat someday.”

“I don’t mean that…what else do you see…in her hair?”

“Oh, flowers,” remarked Harry.

“What kind of flowers do you see?” he asked Harry, displaying a pleased look on his face.

“How should I know? I’m not very good at lobotomy. Shall I ask her?”

“The word is botany; can’t you tell they are chrysanthemums?"

“Chrysanthemums? Never heard of them.”

“Don’t your folks have a garden?”

“Nope, we live in an apartment, but my mom has a few tomato plants.”

“You’ve never seen a real cow,” he responded in exasperation, “and you’ve never heard of chrysanthemums. You’ve lived a rather sheltered life, wouldn’t you say?"

“Yeah, my parents keep me locked up in my room whenever I’m in the house,” muttered Harry.

"Oh, a wise guy, huh?" replied a red-faced and angry Mr. Kennelworth. "Where do you think you're going?" he barked and used language that sent Harry racing for the door.

"To find a cow with chrysanthemums in its hair!"

That was the last conversation Mr. Kennelworth and Harry ever had

29

Tickle the Ivories

Yes, my love for baseball and my love for music often operated simultaneously, and they were frequently in conflict. Baseball practice began right after school at 3 p.m. We were released at 2:15 p.m. and I, in my baseball uniform, ran to my piano teacher's home. Mr. Enright, who lived near Depew Park, gave me a 30-minute piano lesson each week. After finishing the lesson, I ran to the park to practice with the team. Realizing I was going to attend music school in Potsdam, New York, I felt that I required help with my piano skills since I had none. My parents purchased an old Gulbransen piano for $20. A friend of my dad's, also a furniture mover, said that folks were moving to Florida and didn't want the piano. I struggled through lessons and finally got to where I could play most songs in any key, but without all the fancy embellishments that professional pianists seem to so flawlessly exhibit.

Mr. Enright was a gentle soul and a good pianist. He also directed the choirs at our high school. His encouragement came at a time when I needed it.

I will always remember the plaque he had above his piano by William Ward which read: "Flatter me, and I may not believe you. Criticize me, and I may not like you. Ignore me, and I may not forgive you. But encourage me, and I'll never forget you!

SHUSH!

Every time I sauntered into our school library, I felt uncomfortable about the unnaturalness of the atmosphere. It was like a funeral parlor without the music. We were ordered to be quiet and not even allowed to whisper to each other. It was not a place where I cared to hang out.

Miss Ida Hannaway was the typical old maid librarian who constantly raised her index finger to her wrinkled lips. "Shush" Her library was like a mausoleum. She was a cold and distant presence, seldom seen and never to be disturbed. Unfortunately, I have heard of folks that do not allow anyone to sit or walk in their living or dining rooms. These house museums always make me feel uncomfortable.

Later, when I attended music school in Potsdam, I was delighted that the young librarian's philosophy was that there are almost no places where we can attain absolute quietness in our lives. Therefore, she encouraged us to become skilled listeners and develop habits of concentration with a normal conversation going on around us. To this day, I am thankful to Miss Amphora for allowing me to learn to study under normal circumstances.

FAVORITISM

Getting back to baseball, Mr. Lesourde was my baseball coach and my physics teacher. He gave me a good grade in physics because I was a good outfielder. I'm glad he didn't grade my hitting! Even though I was not a great hitter, he played me every game, no doubt, due to my fielding talents in the outfield. Mr. Lesourde was amiable, talkative, and easily distracted from teaching the subject matter at hand.

However, we had to coax him out of his periodic fits of the "blues" after our team lost a baseball game. On a day following a baseball game, Mr. LeSourde would discuss our mistakes for at least half of the physics class. When the team won, he would spend most of the class period talking about how well we played.

I think that he was distracted so much that we probably learned only about half the content of the physics curriculum, along with lots of trivia about baseball. I did, however, pass the New York State Regents Exam in Physics by the skin of my teeth.

How Will You Vote?

"The mediocre teacher tells. The good teacher explains.
The superior teacher demonstrates. The great teacher inspires."
- William Arthur Ward.

Mr. Miller was a clever, creative, bright, bustling, and feisty man who always generated excitement in American History class. He was short, energetic, and forever offered witty one-liners. He challenged us to think for ourselves.

In one specific poignant moment in class, Mr. Miller said, "It's amazing the stuff we accept because that's what we've always been told. For example, in 1490, all the leading scholars examined the plans of Christopher Columbus and wrote, 'Impossible.' They *knew* the Earth was flat; it wasn't open to debate. That is until the little Santa Maria set sail, and the Earth turned out to be round. The impossible became possible because somebody dared to challenge 'conventional wisdom.' We must beware of flat-Earth thinkers."

Another enlightening example cited by Mr. Miller, "Early in this century, America's most influential scientific journal stated, 'Time and money are being wasted on something called aircraft experimentation. Men were never meant to fly.' But one week later, the Wright Brothers taxied their crackpot idea down a homemade runway at Kitty Hawk and launched us all into the air." He then remarked, "Significance should be your goal in life, not survival."

Going to his class was like looking forward to lunch. His presentations were lucid and winning, but at times, we felt he tended to exaggerate, pushing his claims too far. He fielded questions from the students like a professional baseball player with a golden glove.

On a blustery afternoon in late autumn, Mr. Miller was reviewing what was taught during the last class period by asking us lots of probing questions. Suddenly two students abruptly entered the room. He immediately seized the moment and asked them how they planned to vote on the issue at hand. They appeared to be puzzled and shrugged their shoulders as Mr. Miller cleverly brought them into the conversation.

He immediately divided the class into the U.S. House of Representatives and the U.S. Senate. We had debates with opening and closing arguments leading to a vote regarding whether or not Tommy Hughes should be allowed to dye his hair green for St. Patrick's Day. I felt I was back once again in my Jr. High School core group.

"If he did dye his hair, he'd be doing it just to draw attention to himself," bellowed Brad Richmond.

"Yeah, a real sign of immaturity," chirped Phoebe Maguire as she stuck her tongue out at Brad.

Mr. Miller listened attentively to our argument's pros and cons, and took copious notes.

"Who wants to have green hair?" blurted out Bruce Hurt, the big jock.

"I do," yelled Rosie DeCrenza

"Save that statement for when you get hitched," cried Charlie Hunt, which caused the entire class to whoop and yell

"Tommy has the perfect right to dye his hair green if he wants to," stated Mark Jacoby. "He'll look a little weird, but we could get used to it."

"Just like we got used to his weird personality," interrupted Roger Nixon.

Again, the class erupted in laughter while Tommy smirked.

"Yeah, there's no law against having green hair," Ron Chestnut blurted out.

"That's too bad. If we vote 'yes,' you're gonna get green hair," Bruce Hurt said with a sneer.

That remark caused a volcanic eruption of laughter and shouts in the classroom.

We would yell, cajole, stamp our feet, and display other forms of displeasure with comments coming from the floor. The debate raged on and on, with both sides offering their reasons, and at times the debate was so heated that Mr. Miller had to step in and close it down.

Mr. Miller summed up the day's events, "The moment insult, abuse, and threats enter into an argument, it ceases to be an argument and becomes a contest in bitterness. If in an argument we become angry and we resort to wild words and hot threats, then all we prove is that our case is too weak to be stated."

Believe me; Perry Mason and Matlock never had it so good. When we left that class, we were so infused with adrenalin that it took us halfway through the next class to calm down.

Mr. Miller may have been forty. He could pack a punch of enormous rhetorical power in the space of a few words. Mr. Miller taught the basic concepts of American History in a probing and analytical way that has profoundly influenced my teaching and my life

30

THE BEST OF BOTH WORLDS

One of my most memorable students was Vinnie Gasbarra. He had a contagious attitude that spilled over into everything he did. He loved all kinds of music, and he was an excellent drummer.

Vinnie was also a big, lumbering jock who played tackle on the high school varsity football team.

It was 1961, and my first year of teaching at Peekskill High School. Vinnie was a senior who played bass drum in the marching band. I understand he was as aggressive on the football field as he was playing the bass drum in the marching band.

The only potential problem I could foresee was that he played football on Saturdays, and we also performed during halftime at the same football games.

"Vinnie," I said, "it's too bad that there's not two of you, so both the team and the band can benefit from your talent."

"Mr. C, maybe I can work it out," he replied.

At that remark, I didn't fully understand what he was getting at.

He approached me later, during band rehearsal and said, "Coach Devins said I could do both."

"How can you do both band and football on the same day?" I asked.

"Easy, I'll play football for the first half of the game," he said, "and play bass drum in my football uniform for the half-time show, and then go back to play football for the second half of the game."

That's exactly what he did. For nine games, he played both football and marched in the band. He was the hero of both worlds. The local newspaper picked up the story and splashed a picture of Vinnie playing the bass drum in his football uniform on the front page. The title read, "Football and Band Superhero!"

Vinnie went on to be a fine big-band drummer and jazz drummer. He still plays regularly with the finest musicians in the New York area. I think he returned his football uniform.

WATER MY FLOWERS

Most of my Catholic friends attended church on Sundays. We strolled along Washington Street and joined a crowd of people on their way to the local Catholic Church. My uncle Vinnie Fisher lived on Washington Street and rarely attended church, but he could be seen every Sunday morning, watering can in hand, watering his artificial flowers, waving and smiling as the crowd passed by. To him, this was the best part of his week. A handful of people knew the flowers were not real, but they never let on to that fact. I have to admit he did change the flowers according to the season, so he wasn't dishonest about it.

My uncle Vinnie had an out-of-the-ordinary sense of humor. One time he approached me, laughing aloud. I asked him what was so funny.

"I just invented a new deodorant," he said.

"Is it easy to use, and does it smell good?" I asked.

"You spray it on your body, and you disappear," he remarked.

"Disappear?"

"Yeah, everyone stands around and wonders who smells."

I'm sure he walked clockwise!

JUMP AND JIVE

Most of us, who grew up in the 1950s, remember the television show *Happy Days,* where Richie Cunningham, Fonzie, and friends frequented the local soda fountain gathering place. Ours was adjacent to the local bowling alley. It was owned and operated by Frank Ceriale and Rosie, who liked being with young people. Music emanating from the jukebox, dancing in the aisles, ice-cream floats, dates, going steady, bobbysoxers, hamburgers, and the like made this a very special place for us. We frequented this place during lunch, after school, and after Saturday football games. This was a 1950s meeting place for teens; no fights, no drugs, and devoid of trouble.

It seems as though these "Happy Days" are gone forever. I tried to describe to my three children what it was like growing up in the 1950s, and they thought it would be great to experience that.

Campaign Promises

When I was a senior in high school, I ran for president of the high school. While preparing for the candidate's forum in which we would present our ideas and platform for the next school year, in April I discovered from the director of building and grounds, that our old (warm and metallic-tasting) water fountains would be replaced by spanking new electric ones spewing fresh, cold water. The old fountains would be replaced during the summer. Therefore, in my political campaign speech in May, I confidently promised the student body that I would obtain new water fountains for the entire school. I easily won the election. We got the new water fountains for the start of the new school year. Vince, the hero, could have run for the city water commissioner's job.

Boys Will Be Boys

At SUNY Potsdam, there was a lake near the college. We had a history professor named Dr. Winfield, who had an elephant's foot that he used for a waste basket. We thought it was very cool and had fun throwing our folded-up papers in it. One night a group of us sneaked into Dr. Winfield's room and snatched the elephant's foot wastebasket.

We rigged a pulley, ropes, and a hoist extending from the college to the lake. We attached one of my friends, Tommy Tedesco, to the hoist and placed the elephant's foot in his two hands. We moved Tommy along on the hoist, and he would slam the elephant's foot into the ground, spacing them as if an elephant walked into the lake.

The next day, the groundskeeper found the footprints and alerted the administration, who, in turn, contacted the local animal control unit. They came and inspected the footprints, and readily agreed that an elephant must be in the lake. They were going to get their retrieval equipment to drag the lake for the elephant when we came forward and told them what we did. The administration was not amused, and they gave us some extra duties for a week, while the animal control folks said it was an ingenious idea and were glad we came forward.

ALWAYS BE PREPARED

I was a member of the Varsity Dance Band while at Potsdam. We performed for college parties and dances, and occasionally, we performed for off-campus events. We were invited to perform at McGill College in Montreal, Canada, which was located about an hour and a half from Potsdam. We loaded our 18-piece band and two vocalists on the bus and headed to the border to cross over to Canada. When we got to the border, the border patrol told us we couldn't bring our instruments into the country. When we asked why, they responded that we might try to sell them. So, the leader told us to put our mouthpieces and reeds into our pockets. He then phoned ahead to McGill College, explained the situation, and asked if they could have four trumpets, four trombones, five saxophones, and four rhythm section instruments available for us. They agreed. We arrived and immediately took the instruments into the practice rooms to play them. We then ate dinner and played a great concert.

WHICH MAJOR SHOULD I TAKE?

I was the first saxophone major at Potsdam. Like my dad, my teacher Ted Bachelor was a saxophonist in the big bands in New York. At the time being a jazz player was not encouraged, and a saxophonist was taught to be a classical performer. My interest was in becoming a better sax player, but my heart was in playing contemporary jazz like Charlie Parker, Stan Getz, Sonny Stitt, Zoot Sims, and Art Pepper. My lessons were legitimate, and I learned a lot. The college had a rule that one could not change majors unless he could play an audition at a certain level of proficiency. Because I could read music so well, Mr. Bachelor gave me the "Glazunov Concerto for Saxophone" to play at my first recital. It is a beautiful piece but very demanding technically. I learned it and passed my recital, and changed my major to clarinet at the end of my freshman year. I believed I had to learn the clarinet well to teach music.

A Big Opportunity

During my second year, one of my music buddies was leaving college to go play trumpet with the Les Elgart Big Band. He told me they were looking for a lead alto sax player and asked if I wanted to go on the road with the band. I was excited about the prospects of playing with all professionals and traveling throughout the country, but that meant dropping out of college. I phoned my parents and told them about the opportunity. My dad wrote me a letter expressing that I should stay and complete my college education; that I could always play after I finish college or in the summers. That was the only letter I ever received from my dad, and I am sorry I did not keep it. I followed his advice and turned down the opportunity to finish my BS degree in music. I never regretted my decision.

My Second Chance

While teaching music at Peekskill High School, I had another opportunity to play with a top jazz band.

My buddy Tony Salvatori asked if I wanted to play lead alto with the Buddy Rich big band, which was going to tour Japan.

I was married with two children at the time, and my response was, "Wow, Tony, what a great opportunity. I would love to play during the summers, but full-time playing would mean I would have to leave my teaching job and my family."

Was I disappointed? Not really. I was playing most weekends with my combo while enjoying my teaching job and my family. Sure, playing a tour of Japan with the Buddy Rich band would have been sensational musically and would certainly enhance my achievements, but at that point in my life, it would have meant too much of a change.

BE PROACTIVE

My dad always told me that to succeed, you must be proactive and do something to attain your goals, but don't be obnoxious, arrogant, or pushy. The first day I arrived at SUNY Potsdam, we had to get into a line and sign up for classes. Seizing the opportunity, I canvassed all 350 students and asked each who played a jazz instrument. I found a pianist, Bob Boyd, a bass player, Ed Bowman, and a drummer Fred LaBeck. I asked them to rehearse together in the band room that night at 7 p.m. We fit together well and prepared an hour concert. We told everybody about the concert, and we played in the student lounge for an hour that evening for a big crowd.

We stayed together for four years and played many gigs in Potsdam and at Plattsburg State University in Plattsburg, New York, about 90 miles away.

RETAIN YOUR SENSE OF HUMOR

Hank Stampf, a great trombone player who played with the Buddy Morrow and Ray McKinley bands, entered Potsdam as a student. He and I became great friends, and he joined our four-piece band. We traveled to Plattsburg to play a gig at the university. It was a dance with an under-the-sea theme. All kinds of fish were floating around in the air on mobiles and a two-foot pond was directly in front of the band.

Hank did a bit where he put his trombone on the floor and sang and danced to an up-tempo blues song. At one point, he jumped up and down, somewhat like Cab Callaway used to do. However, he became too excited and jumped too high and too far and landed on his back in the pool. He sat up with a large, stupid grin on his face, and looked at me. I calmly reached into my pocket, took out a Lifesaver candy and threw it to him. He laughed heartily with us, and we never forgot that incident.

IMITATION MUSIC?

Nothing upsets me more than seeing artificial fruit, imitation brick or stone, and copying how others play music so one can sound like them. The real thing is tastier (fruit), more tangible (brick and stone), and more convincing (being yourself and knowing who you are).

At SUNY Potsdam, we regularly went to a TGIF jazz session at the Arlington Hotel every Friday from 5 p.m. until 2 a.m. The guys from the music department would "sit in" with the combo and play three or four songs, then grab a beer, sit with a girl or with friends, and listen to the players.

One chilly Friday night in October, I took my saxophone and headed to the Arlington Hotel to join in the jam session. While waiting my turn to play, a new freshman student named Horse Laribee stepped up to the stage. He had an alto sax in his hand and told the rhythm section to play "Confirmation," a song that Charlie Parker made famous.

The rhythm section began the introduction, and Horse played the jazz solo exactly as Charlie Parker played it: note for note! Our mouths were wide in amazement that anyone could do this. After the solo, Horse sat down receiving much applause and had a beer. We thought he must be a whiz of a sax player to do what he did.

The next Friday, Horse came back and sat in again. Yes, you guessed it, He played "Confirmation" again, ala Charlie Parker, note-for-note. By this time, one of my buddies approached Horse and asked if he knew any other songs.

Horse replied with a smile, "No, that is the only song I learned."

We were aghast! How could this be? After further investigation, we learned that Horse couldn't even play an improvised solo on the basic 12-bar blues progression.

I often wondered why anyone would go to all that trouble to copy someone else's solo and not be able to play anything else. I guess he just wanted to impress us and the girls. I think he left school the next semester.

While teaching at Peekskill High School, I attended the National Music Educator's Convention in Nashville, Tennessee. One of the sessions featured the music of the great saxophonist John Coltrane.

The name of the presenter was Andrew White, saxophonist.

Andrew began playing a song, "My Favorite Things," recorded by John Coltrane, exactly like Coltrane played it, note for note. All of the songs were exact duplicates of how Coltrane recorded them. I thought I was back in the Arlington Hotel going through that agonizing experience of listening to Horse Laribee again. While I was amazed at Andrew White's proficiency and his memory of Coltrane's music, I couldn't help but think why someone would want to do something like this. For novelty? To gain an audience? To show off dexterity?

When the concert was over, I turned to my college roommate, Curt Finney, sitting next to me, and said, "I wonder what Andrew White plays like?"

Since then, I have often seen other players trying to imitate the playing of others. Beatlemania is a case in point. They even try to look like the Beatles! Imagine all the guys who try to look like Elvis Presley. Some have even gone so far as to obtain plastic surgery to look like Elvis!

In discussing this with Dad, he pointed out that God created us all different from one another: i.e., distinct fingerprints, personalities, and talents, and it's our job to find out what our talents are and to develop them in the best possible way.

I thought back to when I was just getting into improvising. How I listened and tried to sound like Stan Getz, Lee Konitz, Art Pepper, and

Paul Desmond. I did sound a bit like them at the start, but as I progressed, I developed my style of playing.

My dad's comments regarding one trying to look like someone else. "Maybe I will have plastic surgery done to my face, so I can look like Christopher Columbus and discover another America."

We both had a hearty laugh.

Star Pupils

Upon completing a teaching career of 45 years, I have had the pleasure of teaching music to thousands of students. Instilling the love of music and the joy of living has always been my goal with all my students. Four of my students decided to perform professionally for their living, and three of them continue to do so to this day.

They are Alan "Chip" White (drummer, composer, poet), Michael Cochrane (pianist, composer, author, and educator), Ray Blue (saxophonist, composer, educator), and Professor Louie and the Chromatix (keys, accordion, vocals).

Chip White was an excellent drummer and played many years with Houston Person, saxophonist, along with Jaki Byard, Candido, John Abercrombie, and others.

While teaching at Peekskill High School, I invited four of my students to come with me to hear the Count Basie Band at Birdland in New York City. They had heard the Basie band on recordings, but this was their first time hearing them in person. When we reached Birdland, I told each of them that we would all be drinking ginger ale or cola, and take your time sipping it.

The impact of the Basie band was immediate and lasting, due to the precision playing and rhythmic groove the band created.

Sonny Payne was the drummer and Joe Williams was the vocalist. Just before the Basie band's first song, Pewee Marquette, a little person in a tuxedo, gave a long introduction to the band. Later, I found out from a friend who performed many times at Birdland that Pee Wee gave the band a big introduction if they paid him $20 before the gig began. If not, he merely introduced them with a short mention of their name. What a devious way to make extra money!

Michael Cochrane, pianist, composer, arranger, and educator, recorded and played with Sonny Fortune, Tom Harrell, Clark Terry, Michael Brecker, and Ted Curson, and appeared at the Blue Note, Carnegie Hall, and Alice Tully Hall. He teaches at Rutgers University and two other universities, and has produced over 10 CDs as a leader. Ray Blue, saxophonist, composer, and educator has played with both Chip White and Michael Cochrane. He has toured Europe and Africa with his quartet. He has also performed with Gary Bartz, Benny Powell, the Sun Ra Arkestra, Edie Henderson, and others, and represents the Selmer and VanDoren music companies. Ray has produced several CDs under his leadership.

Professor Louie and the Cromatix...the leader's name is Aaron "Chickie" Hurwitz, a keyboardist, accordionist, and vocalist. His group averages 150 shows per year. Chip White passed away in 2020, while the others continue to bring a high level of music to the public.

I was honored when Ray Blue and Professor Louie nominated me to be a member of the Blues Hall of Fame in 2013. We had a gala concert at the Paramount Theatre in Peekskill with hundreds of blues fans attending. It was a moment to remember as I got a chance to play with Ray Blue and his quartet and with Professor Louie and the Chromatrix. My family attended and loved it!

One former student of mine, Raymond T. Grant, was the solo clarinetist with the Peekskill High School concert and marching bands and has since served as executive director of Robert Redford's Sundance Resort. Prior to his Sundance work, he was artistic director of the Olympic Winter Games in Salt Lake City, Utah. He is also executive producer of arts and culture at a resort in Santa Fe called Bishop's Lodge. Ray lives in Salt Lake City, Utah.

Another music student who excelled after graduating from high school was George Pataki. He played trumpet in the marching and concert bands, and his enthusiastic attitude had a positive influence on the other band members. George became Mayor of Peekskill, New York in 1981, a member of the New York State Assembly from 1985-1992, a member of the New York State Senate from 1993-1994, and went on to become the Governor of New York State from 1995-2006. His accomplishments were many.

Several other notable students include:

- Richard Eisenberg, Peekskill High School marching band, concert band, jazz ensemble - trumpet and piano in New York City.
- Margaret Davies, Drum Majorette for the Peekskill High School marching band. She became a Rockette dancer at Radio City Music Hall in New York City.
- Carl Lerario, tenor saxophonist, Peekskill High School marching band, concert band, and jazz ensemble. Carl is the owner of a music store in Massachusetts.
- David Banta, music arranger, pianist, and recording engineer. He has worked with Michael Jackson, Tina Turner, and Luther Vandross, and produced music for NASCAR, Justin Bieber, Disney, Pixar, Sony Music, and Epic Records.

31

THE FUTURE

"Only the educated are free."
- Epictetus

I have always been uncomfortable in hot weather. When I was born, there was no air conditioning in Peekskill Hospital, and I loudly complained. Seeing how I was unable to speak any intelligible words, my complaints fell on deaf ears. Instead, I heard responses such as, "Isn't he cute?", "He looks like his mother," and "What a darling child."

There wasn't much I could do about it, so I suffered in the heat and toughed it out like all the other babies in the room.

Many years later, my aversion to heat extended to our two trips to Kona, Hawaii, where I taught musical theatre at the University of the Nations. I also found Hong Kong to be uncomfortably hot in the summer.

When I began teaching in Elizabeth City, North Carolina, I again found the heat oppressive. I found it difficult to muster the energy to do anything creative in hot weather.

However, when I attended college at the Crane School of Music in Potsdam, New York, the weather was quite different from that of Hong Kong, Hawaii, or North Carolina.

There were days when the temperature plummeted to 42 degrees below zero. The university's public relations department touted the fact that Potsdam had a dry climate. I thought dry meant little snow and a moderate climate. I was wrong on both counts.

Most Saturday mornings, bassist Ed Bowman, pianist Bob Boyd and I ventured to Plattsburg, New York, about 90 miles from Potsdam. There we teamed with a drummer, Bill Light, who lived in Plattsburg, and we performed at the student union on Saturday afternoons and at a jazz club called Miron's on Saturday nights.

Often, we had no transportation and were forced to hitchhike the 90 miles from Potsdam to Plattsburg, carrying my tenor saxophone and Ed carrying his bass. Bob Boyd didn't need a piano because there was one at both places where we were to perform. Bob lived in Peru, New York, which is near Plattsburg, and went home for the night.

On two occasions, in warm weather, Bob Boyd invited us to stay over at his home, and we picked apples (at 10 cents a bushel and had to clean the entire tree before going on to the next one). The bosses told us we could eat as many apples as we wished. After three or four, I couldn't eat them anymore. Apple picking was okay, but picking peaches was the pits! (Pun intended). Same deal; 10 cents a bushel and clean the whole tree before going on to the next tree. However, peaches have something that apples do not have…fuzz! We itched and scratched and were tortured for a full six hours. Yes, we ate five or six peaches, and that was all we could handle.

Years later, while teaching music at The King's College in Briarcliff Manor, New York, I was addressing an eager group of fifteen freshmen in Music Theory I class. The first thing was to find out the names of each student and where they were from. A pretty, red-haired girl responded, "My name is Phyllis Burch, and I'm from Peru."

"Ah." I said, "I remember picking apples and peaches in Peru" She looked at me with a puzzled gaze and asked, "You picked apples and peaches in Peru?" "Yes." I replied, "After picking peaches for six hours, I itched another six hours while I drove home." By now, the class was beginning to snicker.

"A six-hour drive from Peru?" she asked, as she began to blush and chuckle.

"Yes," I replied. "It's located right outside of Plattsburg, New York."

She looked at me with a shy grin and quietly said, "I'm from Peru, South America."

From that day, I never assumed anything that appeared to be obvious to me.

You may wonder why we traveled so often to Plattsburg when we could have played jazz gigs in Potsdam. The real reason… girls! Plattsburg University had a ratio of seven girls to every boy, and when we arrived, we were treated like celebrities with female groupies.

Occasionally, we got a ride halfway to Plattsburg and had to wait in a diner until a car came along. When the temperature was below zero, we took turns, ten minutes each, standing near the road with our thumbs pointing toward Plattsburg until a car stopped.

After the jazz gigs, Ed and I had a few drinks with some girls, necked a bit, and slept in the boy's dorm. It was great fun as we had our pick of girls. A female smorgasbord! We traveled to Plattsburg intermittently for three years.

One evening, I ventured outside the Delta Kappa fraternity house. It was 42 below zero and dry, so I carefully placed a scarf around my face, cautiously covering my nose and mouth. I could hear the telephone wires creaking and groaning. It was an eerie feeling for the fifteen minutes I remained outside.

Most of us don't like extreme weather, but I prefer cool weather to hot weather anytime. My creative production level is so much more effective in cooler weather.

My First Teaching Job

Following my graduation from Potsdam with a B.S. Degree in Music Education, I taught for one year in East Hartford, Connecticut. My choice of music and my organizing a marching band differed significantly from what the students had experienced before.

After the initial shock of new and fresh ideas wore off, the students became energized and excited about the innovative approach. I added a lot of pizzazz to the half-time formations at football games, and we played a good blend of up-to-date, contemporary music in each show.

My first trumpet player, Lyle Henly, immediately challenged me. Lyle was a fine musician studying with the principal trumpet player of the Hartford Symphony. Lyle could play all music with little effort, had a great tone, and had a powerful playing range. He towered above the others musically and physically with his 6'2" frame. Lyle was seen as a vital person in the band, a real leader.

His less-than-impressive attitude toward marching, refusal to play during field practices to save his lip, his showing up late for band performances, and sometimes leaving early, left much to be desired in my mind.

The truth was that the band depended on Lyle for its tone production and projection of sound on the field. Without him, the band sounded weak and somewhat anemic.

The customary band schedule had band members arriving between 9 and 9:30 a.m. on the day of a home game. They would dress in their band uniforms and be ready to rehearse on the field by 10 a.m. I warmed up and tuned the band, playing scales and chords. At 9:45 a.m., my band managers took attendance.

After giving last-minute instructions to the band, we ventured outside in band formation and marched to the football field. We rehearsed the pre-game show, followed by the half-time show. I never let them play full strength during game-day rehearsals to save their lips for the performance.

Promptly at 10 a.m., the band was in uniform, in formation, on the field, ready to play through the half-time routine, except Lyle. He was nowhere in sight.

Therefore, we practiced without Lyle. Our playing sounded weak and lacking in resonance and projection.

At 10:30 a.m., Lyle showed up, walking toward me. His uniform was thrown over his shoulder, and his trumpet was in its case. He stopped directly in front of me. "Lyle, you know you were supposed to be here by 9:30, in full uniform. What happened?"

He replied, "I dunno; I guess I overslept."

The band was attentively listening to our conversation. I could tell they were wondering what I would do about Lyle breaking the rules on game day.

"Lyle," I said, "take your trumpet and go home. We don't need you today. When you apologize to the band for your bad attitude, then I will let you back in the band."

Lyle was stunned, and his mouth dropped. He certainly believed he was indispensable to the band and that we couldn't play without him. The band members stood silent. Lyle shrugged his shoulders and walked off the field.

Beverly, the drum major and official leader of the band, approached me and remarked, "Mr. Corozine, what you did may not make our band sound better, but it taught us a good lesson about attitude and responsibility."

We performed our half-time show without Lyle. The morale of the band was high, and we got through the show enlivened by the enthusiastic applause of the crowd.

On another occasion, the band worked on a particularly challenging half-time show for a home game. However, it poured rain that day. The game was still on, and I was in the band room talking with the band as the rain pelted against the band room windows. Usually, I dismissed them on days like that.

However, the entire band voted unanimously to perform the half-time show on the field wearing raincoats. I was amazed they wanted to do it. I told the saxophones, clarinets, and flutes to leave their instruments in their cases in the band room. The excessive moisture could potentially ruin woodwind pads and corks and rust the springs.

The brass players and drummers led the band into a fun-filled half-time show. To top it off, pictures of the band performing that afternoon in raincoats appeared on the front page of the local newspaper on Monday. The students were elated.

Lyle showed up on time for practice on the Monday following the incident and apologized to the band for his bad attitude.

I learned early in my career that teaching music is more than teaching the right notes. Training about life through the example we set touches the lives of our students.

Following that year, I enlisted for the draft (everybody had to serve at least two years at that time). Happily, I auditioned for and was accepted into the West Point Band.

During my two years in the United States Army, Mr. Shulman, my high school band director, suffered a heart attack. The Peekskill school district contacted those in authority at West Point and explained the urgency of the situation. They requested that I be permitted to teach at the high school, replacing Mr. Stillman. Much to my astonishment, the supervisors at West Point approved the request, and I was released from the Army two days a week to teach instrumental music at the junior and senior high schools (perhaps my soldiering was worse than my baseball hitting).

I taught for the remainder of that school year, and I was hired for the next school year as a full-time music teacher. I was to work closely with Mr. Shulman as he recuperated. This experience profoundly changed my life. Mr. Shulman did the bulk of the planning, and I carried out the strategies with the band doing most of the physical work. I was directly responsible for implementing the field formations and half-time shows.

During our eleven years together, I learned a great deal about designing half-time shows and what is important in life.

32

THE WORLD STANDS STILL

While teaching at the high school, I would often drive to town at noon and purchase a sandwich at Sammy Chefalo's Grill. Luddy Possente, a traffic police officer, was a close friend of both my brother Nick and me. Whenever Luddy saw me driving through the town, he would stop traffic in all four directions for about three minutes, approach my car and ask me to tell him a joke. This happened regularly, about two or three times a week. Maybe I should have run for mayor and promised to keep everybody laughing with my jokes.

FAST FOOD

Mrs. Needleman was a petite, effervescent woman who ran our school cafeteria like a captain of a ship obsessed with "getting it right." She was indeed a real neatness freak. Erudite, ever-charming in her ways, she was forever instructing us how to use proper table manners, "You must eat all your food. An empty plate is a sign of a good appetite."

She would offer this statement and others like it without provocation and quickly dispense these "gems of wisdom," free to all who would listen. Today, I believe what Mrs. Needleman had to say about eating properly was right.

One day I presented her with a clean, empty plate and asked, “Is this a sign of a good appetite?” She didn’t think much of my remark and frowned as I smiled with a stupid grin on my face.

Casting Impressions

Two impressionable events deeply influenced my life. The first occurred during high school when I attended a concert at the White Plains County Center and listened to the Stan Kenton Big Band. The cascading trumpets, the dramatic and powerful chords for brass, the supple saxophone playing, and the brilliant soloists, combined with an aggressive rhythm section, were incredible.

The other event was a year later. I took a date to New York City to see my first Broadway show, *Guys & Dolls*. Watching Stubby Kaye, Vivian Blaine, and Robert Alda perform live on stage. What excitement. Dancing, comedy, choreography, costumes, and pizzazz. This show has influenced my taste in musical theatre to this day.

Not In There!

While in college, I worked stocking shelves at a local supermarket. On Friday evenings, I brought my tenor saxophone to the store and hid it in the rear of the store behind the wooden slats in the produce department where the eggplants resided. Ralph Manfredi, the produce manager asked, “Vincenzo, whata you doin’ with your saxophone? You gonna serenade the eggplants? I laughed and told him that I was going to play at Green’s Lounge after work. He looked flushed and remarked, “Momma mia! Vincenzo, you are pazzo.” *Pazzo*

means "crazy" in Italian. "You will get killed in there. It'sa nota safe. Go homa, and be safe."

I finished work Fridays at 9 p.m. and then walked two blocks to Green's Lounge with my saxophone in hand. Green's Lounge was about two blocks from the supermarket. It was a noisy bar lounge frequented by neighborhood Black folks. It was not the type of place where I would bring a date. I found out later that most of my Black buddies were not allowed to go to Green's Lounge.

The band at Green's Lounge was a professional, bluesy, be-bop band and I sat in with them every Friday from 9 p.m. to 2 a.m. At 2 a.m., I walked the two miles or so to my home with my sax in hand. My parents were cool about my love of playing. They saw that I never came home inebriated, bummed out, or beat up in any way. I learned long ago that performing and drinking do not mix. When a person drinks, he or she only thinks that they play better. In actuality, they usually sound worse under the influence of drugs or alcohol.

There was a 300-pound man, Tiny, who played the piano and rocked back and forth as he played. There was Clyde who blew a mean blues trumpet and played notes higher than I ever heard before. Quiet, unassuming Leon played the upright bass, and never said much. Crazy Tiger dazzled us with his drumming, and by tossing his drumsticks in the air. He also shouted out loud, enthusiastic remarks like, "Yeah man," and "Go for it." The tenor saxophone player at Greene's Lounge was Junior Blood Guts. He was about 5 feet tall, wore a porkpie hat, sported a goatee, and used jazz lingo such as "Man," "Cool," "Crazy," "I can dig it," and other "hip" remarks. Junior let me play every song and he encouraged me to blow my sax with confidence and to project the sound on my horn. What an education! Junior was my hero!

On Friday, I invited my friend and college classmate Ed Bowman, who played string bass and lived in New Rochelle, to meet me at 9 p.m. at the supermarket and to bring along his bass. I told him we would be "sitting in" with a few musician friends.

Ed Bowman was a calm, soft-spoken, mild, conservative guy with a conniving sense of humor. Ed also played great string bass, showed up exactly at 9 p.m., and we went in his car to Green's Lounge. He took one look at the neighborhood and the bar patrons and blurted out, "No way am I going in there; I'm liable to get killed!"

"There's no need to worry," I chuckled. "Follow me and shake everybody's hand as you work your way through the crowd to the bandstand."

Ed was a White guy, who, after assessing the situation in Green's Lounge that evening, was whiter than usual.

All worked well once Ed, and I maneuvered our way to the bandstand, shaking hands and smiling as we went.

Good people who love jazz are good people regardless of their color.

WOW! WE MADE IT ON TV!

In the early 1960s, I began teaching music at Peekskill High School in Peekskill, New York, and was the director of the marching band.

There were approximately 125 members in the band, including twirlers, band managers, and band mascots. Realizing there were only 750 students in the high school, grades 10-12, it is remarkable that so many students joined the band.

At the same time, the New York Jets professional football team held their spring training in Peekskill at the grounds of the Peekskill Military Academy. As you can surmise, the stands were full of admiring fans who came to see the Jets in action!

Joe Namath, the quarterback, put on a great show for the onlookers with his fancy and accurate passing.

As a result of the Jets practicing in our city, the officials of the NY Jets invited our high school marching band to perform a half-time show at the Polo Grounds in NY during a Jets football game for national TV.

Pandemonium broke out! The faculty, administration, and students were stunned by the situation. This was a "wow" moment for all!

Realistically, most of our students had never seen a professional football game, let alone perform a half-time show on national television! The excitement in the school and the city had never been higher. Imagine the Peekskill High School Marching Band performing on national television. This was a very big deal indeed! It equaled the enthusiasm of the election of the President of the United States.

To digress for a moment, our high school band had a reputation for doing precise and intricate field maneuvers. There was no other band in our class that put on a more electrifying half-time show. In fact, for the past two years, no visiting football team brought their band to our home games, and consequently, the band members never had the opportunity to see other bands perform except when we attended away games.

When I was a junior at SUNY Potsdam, my student-teacher assignment was to go to Freeport, New York on Long Island. Freeport had one of the most superb marching bands in the state. With nearly 250 band members from a high school of over 2,000, their sound filled the stadium, and their maneuvers awed the crowd.

Back in the 1960s, I thought our marching band deserved to see other bands that performed at our level, so I went into coach John Devins' office one Monday morning. "John, I have an idea. I was wondering if for next year, you would try to set up a game against the Freeport football team, so we could compare band performances."

John paused, smiled, and said, "For the band, that's a great idea, but for our team, we would get murdered against those big guys." They were two class levels above us, and their players weighed a lot more than our kids. Some of our kids would no doubt get injured as a result. With over 2,000 in their high school, that meant that they had almost 1,000 boys from which to choose, while out of our 750 students, we had only around 350 boys to choose from.

I was disappointed by what he said, but I understood his position. We would have to be satisfied with watching the great bands on television like Ohio State and Grambling State University.

Hurriedly, I arranged the music for the 14-minute half-time show at the Polo Grounds and prepared the band at 7:30 every morning outside in the school parking for three weeks following our regular season. We also had a three-hour rehearsal at Depew Park just before the big day.

Chip White, our talented jazz drummer, was the featured soloist at the game. We placed his drum set on a large platform with a moving dolly and rolled him out to the center of the field, surrounded by the band.

The band was an immense hit, and for the city of Peekskill, we were instant celebrities. The pride in the city and the band was enormous and gratifying. Peekskill Day at the Polo Grounds was a huge success, and the Jets won behind the dazzling throwing of Joe Namath.

Following that game in early December, they tore down The Polo Grounds and began work on the new Shea Stadium in Flushing, Queens, New York.

The superintendent of schools called me into his office and told me about the request from the Jets' front office for our band to again perform, but this time at the new Shea Stadium. I was delighted to hear it. Another half-time show at the spanking new Shea Stadium. The excitement began to swell again in the school and city. Another Peekskill Day was on the horizon! However, I asked the superintendent, "Do you think this is a good idea?"

He looked puzzled and asked, "What do you mean, Vince?"

"Well, after our last appearance at the Polo Grounds, they tore down the stadium. I wouldn't want that to happen again after we perform at Shea Stadium!"

The superintendent hesitated and then began to roar with laughter. "Vince, get out of here."

I was laughing as hard as he was by that time.

The usual procedure for submitting a budget from each department was to submit it to the principal, who, in turn, would review it and pass it on to the superintendent and then to the Board of Education for final approval. My marching band budget was separate from that of the music department, and I submitted it directly to the superintendent and then the Board of Education.

Most budgets were trimmed back, items deleted, questioned, and challenged as to their necessity. But my budget was never challenged after the successes during the two Jets games.

The largest budgets in the school system were physical education and the budget for the marching band. No one ever cut anything out of my budget. They passed it, asking, "How much does Vince need next year for the band?"

The superintendent quoted the amount from my budget submission, and the Board of Education unanimously gave me whatever I asked.

Frank, our orchestra director, learned about my budget capabilities and told me he had asked for a new string bass for the orchestra for three years, and never got it passed. I said, "No problem, Frank. Let me know how much it cost, and I will put it into the marching band budget."

His eyes lit up and he thanked me for helping him. Yes, the budget was passed, and he got his new string bass, even though it is not an instrument normally in a marching band. Clout can shout!

33

THE CONTEST

During my teaching at Peekskill High School, beginning in 1961, I became acquainted with Mr. DeCherry, the Superintendent of Buildings and Grounds. Mr. DeCherry was an insensitive, gruff man who never showed a sense of humor. I believed he had none since I never once saw him smile.

Mr. DeCherry had no patience for anyone or anything out of his range of concern, and he always seemed as though he was late for an appointment. He had little time to talk to anyone. He was good at barking orders.

After working with Mr. DeCherry for a few years, I was convinced he was happiest when the schools were closed and the students and teachers were at home.

Plans were being made to construct a new high school on the historic grounds of the former Peekskill Military Academy. As director of music for the district of Peekskill, I was brought in to review the plans for the new music wing. I offered suggestions. I quickly noticed some glaring omissions in the plans, such as, "Where is the orchestra pit?" "Where are the dressing rooms?" "Where is the prop room?"

I tactfully presented my views on the new music wing, which made Mr. DeCherry mumble under his breath. When I suggested they hire a sound acoustic engineer to design the auditorium and music rooms, I was met with opposition from Mr. DeCherry. "Are you crazy? Do you know how much that will cost?" He scowled and tried to push my suggestions under the table.

However, the Superintendent of Schools, Dr. Rinehart, listened attentively to my comments and motioned Mr. Cherry to seriously consider them. Promptly, Mr. DeCherry wrote my ideas down on a scratch pad he always carried with him, mumbling through it all. After much wrangling about acoustics and soundproofing the recording studio and music wing, I casually mentioned that we would all benefit acoustically and aesthetically if the music wing was curved.

"What! Are you crazy?" bellowed Mr. DeCherry. "Do you know how much that would cost the taxpayers?"

"No, I don't," I calmly replied, "but it would make the building look nice aesthetically, and the sound would be better."

Mr. DeCherry stewed and grumbled under his breath as I excused myself from the meeting. I figured I said enough for one day and didn't want Mr. DeCherry to run me over with his car in the parking lot.

Exactly one month later, I read in the local newspaper that a dispute was rising in the city over the possible removal of the historic "hanging tree" located right where the new high school entrance would be. The tree dated back to the Revolutionary War and was used to hang traitors and dissidents. The city historians rose to the occasion and demanded that the hanging tree be preserved for historical purposes. The City Council got behind the historians as they approached the local school board with their signed petitions. The school board, after much consternation, agreed that the hanging tree would stay intact.

To preserve the hanging tree intact, they had to redesign the plans for the high school and curve the music wing! I won, I won!

After that occurrence, Mr. DeCherry gave me suspicious and disbelieving looks as he grunted something under his breath. I cheerily addressed him in passing. The soundproofing and recording studio were acceptable, but aesthetically we achieved a great deal by curving the building.

To this day, I believe Mr. DeCherry thinks I was instrumental in influencing the historians and the city council to take the action they did so I could win my point!

INTERVENTION

Returning from a lunch break while teaching at Peekskill High School, I noticed a large group of students assembled at the edge of the teacher's parking lot. I sensed a fight was imminent. I quickly drove my car into the middle of the students, got out of my car, and yelled at the top of my lungs, "I want everybody to go back inside the school…now!" They did exactly that. Would I do that today? I don't think so. I was glad, however, to be able to prevent a violent outbreak on that day.

KNOW WHERE YOU LIVE

While attending the Crane School of Music in Potsdam, New York, all teacher candidates were required to complete one semester of student teaching during our junior year at two different locations.

In 1956, I was assigned to Rye High School in Rye, New York, and Freeport High School in Freeport, Long Island, New York. I knew that Freeport had an exceptionally fine marching band, and I learned much from working with them.

While at Freeport, I stayed with a physical education teacher and his family, George Markevitch, who was also the head football coach at the high school. George and his wife Lillian told me they would be away for Christmas vacation and that in the event I returned earlier than they did, I should enter the house through the garage door.

My dad, accompanied by my mom, drove me to Freeport, Long Island. We arrived around 6:30 p.m. It was dark outside, and unfortunately, all the houses looked the same at night.

Therefore, I took my suitcase, lifted the garage door, and went up the cellar stairs to the living room. Upon entering the living room, I yelled, "Wow, the Markevitches got a piano and didn't even tell me. Now I can practice every day at home instead of having to stay late and use the piano at school."

So, I pulled out the piano bench and began to play the piano with gusto. I played for about two hours. Suddenly I looked up, and on the mantle above the fireplace, I saw a photo of a different family. My heart sank. I tried to swallow but couldn't. I carefully and quietly closed the piano cover and slid the piano bench into its original position. Then I grabbed my suitcase and slinked down the stairs to the garage. When I got outside, I checked the house number. I had entered the wrong house. It was the home of their next-door neighbors.

I quickly scampered to the Markevitches house before they arrived home, through the garage, as I was asked to do, and sat in a fluffy chair shaking with the realization that somebody could have been at home next door when I began playing the piano. On the other hand, perhaps the neighbor could have mistaken me for an intruder and shot me dead! After all, I was a trespasser. I suddenly vanished into silent solitude.

It was a long time before I could compose myself and act normal again. My breathing slowed considerably. My chest was pounding. When George and Lillian returned after 11 p.m., I was still sitting in the fluffy chair. I told them what had happened, and they were more amused by my mistake than shocked. They snickered a great deal as I explained my plight and consequent fear.

The next day we all went over to the neighbors, the Mendelssohns, and told them the entire story. The Mendelssohns were understanding and decided not to leave their garage open while away from home.

A Little Prayer Helps

For over fifteen years, I adjudicated musical groups such as concert bands, orchestras, choirs, and jazz bands for various organizations in the greater New York and New Jersey areas. The organizations would invite high school musical groups to New York City and perform for a panel of judges. In return, students would receive a rating and comments for musical improvement. The attraction was that the students could attend a show on Broadway and eat at a restaurant in New York in addition to their performance for the judges.

These concerts were often held at local high schools because they already had percussion equipment, music stands, risers, chairs, performing stages, and one or two pianos. The festival would begin at 8 a.m. and end around 6 p.m. A panel of four to six judges would sit together in the rear of the auditorium writing comments on a small desk, using a tape recorder to record verbal comments which were later given to the directors of the musical organizations to share with their students.

During one of these festivals, an orchestra from Iowa was listed to play. None of the other judges volunteered to work with orchestras; most were directors of bands or choruses, so none of them wanted to take the task of adjudicating and working with an orchestra. Adjudicators worked with each group for 15 minutes on the stage discussing problems and offering suggestions for improving the sound of the group.

The other judges knew I had experience with orchestras, besides my experience with bands and choirs, so they asked me to critique the orchestras on the stage after their presentation.

I agreed, and they all sighed in relief. We listened attentively as the orchestra from Iowa played selections by Ravel, Beethoven, and Bach. We couldn't believe what we heard. Not only did they play these great compositions, but they played them expertly! The judges' mouths were wide open in astonishment. No mistakes!

After the orchestra finished, to the applause of approximately 300 listeners in the audience, I ambled down the aisle carrying my conducting baton. I asked myself, "What can I say to improve a group that played everything perfectly?"

I suddenly thought of what my mother had taught me, "Vinnie, whenever you find yourself in a difficult situation, pray to God for the answer."

I said quietly, "God, you have to help me with this one…I don't know what to do. How can I improve a perfect performance?"

Upon reaching the stairs to the stage, I sensed a new thought, "Play the Bach Fugue and make it dance!"

I got my answer from God, and it was nothing I had ever thought of.

The fugue is the most difficult part of the piece, as the four parts enter at different places, and the music builds to a climax at the end.

I told the students to sit forward on the edge of their chairs and make the fugue *dance*."

The results were remarkable. The piece received new life. I could see their teacher smiling, and they received a standing ovation from the audience. The orchestra conductor told me she never thought of doing what I did, and it opened up new possibilities for her. She even hugged me.

34

My Brother, The Drummer

At home, I had two brothers: Nick, who is 18 months younger, and Richie who is nine years younger. Nick was a solid athlete who played a lot of sports and was a drummer with a few local commercial bands. Richie had a photographic memory and was talented in art. He tried to play trombone while in elementary school, but the trombone slide was too long for his arms, so he gave it up.

Nick and I shared a bedroom, and all hell broke loose if my slippers, socks, or shoes were anywhere near his bed. He drew a line that marked his territory. If I crossed that line, a raucous pillow fight would ensue with lots of yelling and punching. I don't know how my folks put up with us.

Nick and I played sports with our friends, and we got along okay most of the time, as long as I stayed with my friends and him with his. Whenever we chose sides to play a game, Nick didn't want me around.

Nick always remarked, "Don't pick Vinnie. He has to go home and practice his sax at 4:30."

My brother was right. I'd leave at 4:30 to practice until 6 when dinner was ready. So I got picked last, batted last, and played right field, a position that no one wanted to play. Even though I was a good ballplayer, no one wanted me on their team because at 4:30, they would suddenly be without a player…a real disadvantage in sandlot baseball. I was glad to know that it wasn't my ball-playing or personality that kept me out of things.

When I left at 4:30, Nick would yell, "See, I told you so."

Nick went to the State University of New York, at Plattsburg, New York, but after two months, he returned home (he didn't like the food) and went to work for IBM from where he retired.

My youngest brother, Richie, memorized all the information on hundreds of baseball cards and could recite that information freely and accurately to the amazement of our friends. Nick and I used to show off the abilities of our little brother to anyone who happened to be around. It was a Smith Street Circus Side Show.

It wasn't until many years later that we found out that our mom had discarded the thousands of baseball cards that Richie had accumulated when we moved from Smith Street to Requa Street. Today, those baseball cards would enable Richie to buy a new home and a big car.

I was an enthusiastic New York Giants baseball fan, and Nick passionately followed the Brooklyn Dodgers. We fussed and argued vehemently over every statistic on both teams. Sometimes our dad had to intervene to calm us down. One night the Giants were playing the Dodgers, and my dad thought there would finally be some semblance of peace between Nick and me. However, Nick wanted to listen to the broadcast on the Dodger station with Red Barber, and I wanted to listen to the game on the Giant station with Frankie Frisch. After much squabbling, my dad decided that each of us would listen to half the game on each station.

THE AUDITION

During my time in the sixth grade at Franklin Elementary School, I played the saxophone, and my brother Nick was just beginning on the drums.

Mr. Konnerth, the music teacher, asked the band to vote on who played the drums the best. The winner would be allowed to play with the school orchestra. My brother Nick and Nat Ziolkowsky were the two candidates for the drum position. After listening to both play, there was no doubt that Nat Ziolkowski was the better drummer, so I voted for Nat.

Nick was offended that I didn't vote for him; after all, he was my brother. I told him that Nat played better and that he should practice more. Nick didn't speak to me for three weeks following that incident. I tried to talk to him, but he clammed up and made me believe I wasn't even in the same room with him. Even when he ate his usual four peanut butter sandwiches (no jelly) at night, he ignored me.

FRANK, LIZA, AND SAMMY

While directing the very popular Peekskill High School Marching Band, each year, there would be a competition among the girls to see who would be chosen as next year's drum majorette to lead the band.

In the 1960s, a young girl named Margaret Davies tried out for drum majorette and easily won the spot. Margaret was a trained singer, dancer, and an overall beautiful young lady who led the marching band with style and class.

Following high school, Margaret tried out for the Rockettes at Radio City Music Hall in New York City and was chosen as a Rockette. She danced for a few years and married a wealthy magnate who owned large companies, and they had a daughter.

During Margaret's days as a Rockette, she and her husband hobnobbed with many famous people like Frank Sinatra and the Rat Pack, Don Rickles, Telly Savalas, Robert Wagner, Clint Eastwood, and more.

Margaret contacted me some years later and told me about a few things she experienced after graduating. For instance, she was riding in a limo with Frank Sinatra, and Frank told her, "Margaret, if anybody gets fresh with you, tell me, and I will take care of them." She said that Frank was a perfect gentleman and was good to her.

A few years later, through my friends, vocal soloist Mary Mancini and her husband, accordionist Mario Tacca, we met Hank Catangno who was the sound man for Frank Sinatra, Liza Minelli, Sammy Davis, Steve Lawrence, and Eydie Gormé. Hank is a real family man who loves pasta and likes to laugh.

He said that when Frank, Liza, and Sammy performed together, he would have to accommodate the whims and desires of each. Frank and Liza wanted the temperature in their dressing rooms to be exactly perfect for them. One wanted it cooler, and one wanted it warmer, so Hank had to put up cardboard shields over the vents for one and boost the temperature for the other.

Also, Liza wanted certain colored towels in her dressing room while Sammy Davis, a heavy smoker, had to place a pack of Sammy's favorite cigarettes every eight feet around the dressing room and the hall leading to the stage.

I had the pleasure of writing music and conducting for Mary Mancini and Mario Tacca while Hank did the sound at the Garden State Arts Center in New Jersey one weekend.

While my wife Norma and I were at Mary and Mario's home with Hank, he talked freely about his time with Frank. While in Atlantic City, Frank peered out his hotel window, watching the people walk along the street. He mentioned to Hank that he can't even do that; walking on the street without being mobbed by crowds. Even when he went to eat in a restaurant, Frank would sit next to the wall, and he would be surrounded by his bodyguards who would keep the public away from him.

While Frank was still alive, toward the end of his life, I told Hank I always dreamed of arranging for Frank. Hank liked the arrangement I played for him and told me Frank was not doing any new stuff anymore. His memory was slipping, and he needed cue cards to remember the lyrics, and most of his arrangements had been lowered in pitch by a half or whole step because he couldn't sing as high as he once used to.

Hank also mentioned that he preferred not to stay in the same hotel as Frank. I asked why. He said that whenever Frank had a personal need, he called him. One day Frank cut his finger and called Hank to get him a Band-Aid and put it on his finger. He said he and Frank were very good friends, but he needed more peace and tranquility when working.

He told us about how generous Frank is. He often gave money to folks who needed it and told Hank not to tell anyone. Frank had a rough exterior with a tender heart!

FIRST DANCE

When I was a sophomore in high school, Flo Morini, a junior, asked me to accompany her to her junior prom. I was surprised but flattered at the same time. My mom and dad thought I should be polite and accept the invitation.

My folks had to rent a dinner jacket, cummerbund, and bow tie for me. They bought me a new pair of black shoes and a corsage for Flo. After all, I couldn't show up empty-handed. My mom and dad reminded me to be polite and act like a gentleman at the dance. I was a little upset they felt they had to tell me that.

A live band was at the prom, punch and cookies were in abundance, and the gym was decorated with the theme: "Fish of the Sea." All kinds of fish were there—sharks, tuna, squid, octopus, but we could never find Nemo no matter how hard we tried. Even the paper plates had pictures of fish on them. The ladle for the punch bowl was even shaped like a fish. I was thankful that no student had thrown any real fish in the punchbowl. Only plastic ones.

Flo and I danced every dance, and the night was enjoyable for both of us. When we were driven back to Flo's house by her dad, I said goodnight, thanked her and shook her hand. I didn't know if I should kiss her or not, seeing that it was our first date, and I wasn't interested in pursuing a relationship at that age. I also had very little practice in kissing. The handshake seemed to suit her father. He smiled and went inside the house with Flo behind him. Flo waved "goodnight" to me.

Presto! Sleight Of Hand

Most professional recording musicians get paid by the hour, or usually for a three-hour session and by the hour for overtime.

The union scale for a professional musician in Maryland is $900 per person, which includes three rehearsals and one performance. Employing a 60-piece orchestra (30 strings and a total of 30 woodwinds, brass, and percussion), will cost the producer $54,000. Solo singers and dancers receive compensation of around $2,000. Producing a concert with a large orchestra will cost approximately $60,000-$100,000.

Often the arranger/conductor wishes to get a full sound from the string section. It is best to "overdub" or overlay the strings on top of the track they just recorded. During my conducting stints with the Hong Kong Philharmonic Orchestra, this could be done with no extra payments needed for the players, with the stipulation that the producer must provide lunch for all players.

The situation in the U.S. is not so simple. If one wishes to have the string section record overtop (overdub) of the track they played in the United States, each player must receive double pay for that particular session. This can add lots of money to a music project.

I was conducting a jingle project in New York City, and we were using a string section of nine violins, three violas, and three cellos, which can produce a full sound. I wanted the strings to produce a richer sound and I stated that to the engineer, who told me," No problem, Vince, I got it covered."

I began conducting the session, and after the first take with the strings, the engineer said, "Vince, I thought I heard a bow scratch in the strings; let's do another take." I didn't notice it but the engineers can pick up fine points while recording. I asked the strings to record it once more. I didn't give it another thought and then went on to rehearse the next piece. Following the session, I was in the booth with the recording engineer, and he told me to listen to what was recorded. I was stunned! The strings sounded larger than I ever thought they could. I learned that when we re-recorded the strings, he simply recorded it on another track and doubled the string sound without paying the player's double scale.

This "sleight of hand" bothered me, but I didn't feel I could challenge it. It was his studio, and he hired me for the project.

I guess as costs escalate, there are ways to skirt around them and save money.

COUNT WHO?

Two weeks before entering the U.S. Army, I returned home early one evening, opened the front door, and saw my cousin Al. Sitting next to him was a beautiful, petite young girl. Al was dating Norma Salvestrini from Mahopac, New York. He came to see my folks and introduce Norma to them.

I was struck by her beauty, stunning smile, and poise. I promptly phoned her the next day and asked her to go out with me. She accepted, but one day before I was to go into the Army, she phoned and said, "Vin, I'm still going out with Al, and I don't think it's a good idea to see you."

Although disappointed, I thanked her for calling, and the next day I took the train to New York to be inducted into the U.S. Army at Whitehall Street.

After winning another push-up contest, I received my usual weekend pass to go home to play with my jazz band.

On Sunday afternoon, I was conducting an 18-piece jazz band of professional musicians, and we were rehearsing at a local club called the Vagabond Club.

Norma was riding in a car with her three girl cousins, and as they passed the club where I was playing, they saw flashing pizza signs and lots of cars outside. They entered and sat at a table, and ordered pizza. The room was so full of cigarette smoke that I didn't see them.

During one 15-minute break, a high school buddy, Gary Apon, came up to me and said, "Vin, there's a girl over there who knows you."

I looked where he was pointing and saw Norma sitting with her three cousins. I went over and said hello and asked Norma to dance to the music emanating from the jukebox.

While dancing, I asked how she and Al were doing. She said, "Oh, Al and I don't go out anymore."

With a delightful smile, I asked her to go out with me to New York City the next Saturday. I was confident I would win another push-up contest and get another pass home for the weekend.

I easily won the next push-up contest that Friday and headed home at noon. I had a jazz gig Friday night and was free to take Norma out Saturday.

I found 10 Veschi Lane in Mahopac and knocked at the front door. A very pretty lady, Ida, Norma's mom, answered. I next met Leo, Norma's father. He was an ex-Marine, a big domineering person, opinionated, tough, and a drinker of alcohol.

He welcomed me and asked if I wanted a drink. I told him I don't drink much, but he was so insistent that I finally accepted. He poured a shot glass of yellow liquid from a bottle with a wooden branch on it.

I smiled and brought the glass to my lips. After a small sip of this golden brew, I thought my eyebrows would light up! When Leo wasn't looking, I poured the liquid poison into a small plant on the table. I never did find out if the plant died!

Leo owned and ran a restaurant in Mahopac called Skippers and was seldom home. However, when he heard that Norma was going out with a jazz musician, he balked and said, "All musicians are drug addicts!" When Norma explained to him that I was a high school music teacher, he finally agreed to let her go out with me.

Norma was still upstairs getting ready. Leo leaned over to me and said softly, "Norma is my only daughter and is a beautiful one. I want her brought back as nice as she is right now, or I'll break your neck!" (His language was more colorful than that.)

I immediately replied, "What time do you want her home?"

Norma and I dated for three years, and we finally married after my first year of teaching at Peekskill High School in 1961.

She didn't like me at first. She thought I was a know-it-all; opinionated and a wise guy. After all, I was a city kid, and she grew up in the suburbs.

Norma was, and is still, kind, polite, smart, and consistent in her moods. She never complains or demands anything from me and easily adapts to all situations.

The first date I had with Norma, who now is my wife, was when I took her to Birdland in New York City to hear the Count Basie Band. She had never heard of either Birdland or Count Basie. I was amused that she thought Birdland was a bird sanctuary and that Count Basie was a foreign dignitary. After many years of marriage, she has learned a lot about music in general, and especially about jazz. She can even tell when I haven't been practicing and sound a little rusty.

Did You Hear About It?

Humor has the effect of diffusing most tense situations if handled properly.

Jeanne Calment, who was born before the invention of the telephone and the Eiffel Tower, died at the age of 122. She outlived 27 French presidents and entered the Guinness Book of World Records as the oldest woman. When asked about the secret of her longevity, she replied, "Laughter."

Medical science proves that laughter strengthens the immune system, lowers blood pressure, and counteracts the inertia caused by depression. The book of Proverbs states, "A cheerful heart is good medicine."

Research has revealed that children laugh about 400 times a day and adults only about 15.

My tenure at The King's College in Briarcliff Manor, New York, lasted for sixteen years, from 1977-1993. Due to declining enrollment, the school eventually closed its doors in the 1990s.

I have always enjoyed a good laugh and particularly like to tell funny stories and jokes to others to observe the reaction of my "victims" to my joke-telling.

The unofficial "joke chain" operated like this; I would tell a colleague a joke in the morning, and by 1 p.m., all the faculty and staff would hear it. However, if they, in turn, told this joke to another or tried it on their students, they would carefully monitor the response received. A favorable response (chuckle, laugh, or guffaw) would elicit a comment such as, "Yes, that was a good one." An unfavorable response (groan, blank stare, indifference) would invariably bring forth the following response, "Professor Corozine told me that one."

No matter how hard I tried, I couldn't win! My reputation as a joke teller preceded me wherever I went.

"The illiterate of the 21st century will not be those who cannot read and write, but those who cannot learn, unlearn and relearn."
- Alvin Toffler

Before I went to school, I was a kid who laughed a lot.

EPILOGUE

What did I learn from all these experiences? Human beings are as different as snowflakes and as varied as our fingerprints. We are magnificently fashioned to be funny, clever, thoughtful, caring, and creative. Born as originals and not copies of anyone else. Within us are deposited gifts that need to be developed and used to help others and improve their lives.

Each person has their story, and we all carry "baggage" that must be overlooked if we are to coexist on this planet. Having fun with others can be refreshing if the differences do not separate us or polarize us into a protective and self-centered shell. The cultural differences that exist between us are delightful and should be respected.

I take pleasure in observing how people react to different situations and delight in speculating why we respond in certain ways. Realize that we are fully human with obvious character flaws and shortcomings. Laughing *with* each other is a process that will both heal us and make us more human.

Proverbs 17:23: A merry heart is good medicine…

About The Author

"When life handed me a lemon, not only did I make lemonade, but I bought the whole orchard and later sold it for a profit!"

– Me

Vince Corozine was born and raised in Peekskill, New York, in an Italian family that loved great music, good food, and laughter.

He earned three degrees in music and taught at the high school and university levels. He was a musician in the West Point Band and arranged music for The Norm Hathaway Big Band, which appeared at the Iridium Jazz Club on Broadway in New York City and a special appearance on *Saturday Night Live*. His books include *Arranging Music for the Real World* and *Jazzin' the Blues,* published by Mel Bay Music. He is a member of ASCAP, The League of American Orchestras, and the Blues Hall of Fame.

He traveled the world, conducting members of the Toronto Symphony, Hong Kong Philharmonic, Philly Pops, the Kunming Symphony in China, and professional musicians in New York City.

Regardless of the roadblocks set before him, he was able to use his humor and creativity to be a musician. The uncanny ability to turn a negative situation into a positive one has been a plus for him. When doors closed, he went through another or a window. He learned to face the music even when he didn't like the tune.

Check out his website at www.vincecorozine.com
Email: norvin22@verizon.net

Other Works by Vince Corozine

- **Dramatic Dance:** *Toymaker and Son* - 52 minutes of music recorded with members of the Toronto Symphony. Produced in 26 countries.
- ***Creation* musical composition for orchestra and choir** (2022): 28 minutes of music in four movements: I. Galaxy, 2. His Voice is Over the Waters (soprano soloist and orchestra), 3. Creation of Man/ Fall of Man with two dancers, IV. Chorale and Fugue (orchestra and chorus)
- **A New Musical: *A Dream of Wings*** (2022) - The story of the Wright brothers in their quest to fly.
- ***Ba-Ba the Car***: Contemporary dance.
- ***The Rhythm Kings*:** musical about a true story of a "mixed" musical group of teens in the 1950s.
- ***Arranging Music for the Real World*** (2002) - Mel Bay Publications.
- ***Jazzin' the Blues*** (for intermediate pianist, 2018) - Mel Bay Publications.
- **Motivational Speaker/Humorist** - Enjoy Vince's saxophone playing as he relates humorous stories about his life as a mall-walker, as a musician traveling the world as an arranger, composer, and conductor, his time spent at West Point with the band, and his years obtaining an education

An Invite to Write

Did this book help you in some way? If so, I'd love to hear about it. If you wish to write a review about *Encounters with Life*, please post it to Amazon.com. Thank you for reading my book.

- Vince

CPSIA information can be obtained
at www.ICGtesting.com
Printed in the USA
BVHW071538020223
657731BV00006B/219

9 781735 617121